The Leonardo DiCaprio Album

The Leonardo DiCaprio Album

BRIAN J. ROBB

Plexus, London

British Library Cataloguing in Publication Data
  Robb, Brian J.
  The Leonardo DiCaprio album
  1. DiCaprio, Leonardo 2. Motion picture actors and
  actresses - United States - Biography
  I.Title
  791.4'3'028'092

ISBN 0 85965 2424

Cover design by John Mitchell
Book design by Mandy Mitchell
Printed in Great Britain by Jarrold Book Printing, Thetford

10 9 8 7 6 5 4 3

Acknowledgements
We would like to thank the following journalists,
newspapers and magazines whose interviews and articles
on Leonardo were invaluable: 'Great Picture, Leonardo'
by Bart Mills, *You* Magazine (*Mail on Sunday*), August
29th 1993; 'Guns 'n' Poses' by John Clark, *Premiere*,
October 1995; 'What's Eating Leonardo DiCaprio',
Premiere, November 1995; 'In the Raw: David Thewlis'
by Holly Millea, *Premiere*, November 1995; 'The Out
There Brother' by Chris Heath, *The Face*, December
1995; 'I Would Die 4 U' by Christine Spines, *Premiere*,
October 1996; 'Growing Pains' by Sarah Simpson,
Attitude, January 1996; 'Golden Wonder' by David Cox,
i-D magazine, October 1996; 'The Long Brief Encounter'
by Christopher Hampton, *The Sunday Telegraph*, April
6th 1997; 'Demi's Secret Night With Movie Romeo' by
Stuart White, *News of the World,* March 2nd 1997;
'Straight From The Hip' by Giles Whittell, *The Times*
Magazine, March 29th 1997; 'Nineties Romeo' by Craig
McLean, *The Scotsman Weekend*, March 29th 1997.

Other organisations and individuals who helped out
along the way were: the Library & Information Services,
the British Film Institute, Film Publicity Notes and The
Internet Movie Database.

I would like to thank the following magazines and
newspapers for their coverage of Leonardo DiCaprio:
*Interview, Big, Sugar, Mizz, My Guy, Film Review, Punch,
Kerrang!, Live & Kicking, Asian Age, Cosmopolitan, The
Week, Just 17, Detour, Sight & Sound, Variety,
Hollywood Reporter, Empire, Neon, The Village Voice,
Movieline, Time, Entertainment Weekly, People Magazine,
Time Out, The Times, Manchester Evening News, The
Sunday Telegraph, The Daily Telegraph, Irish Sunday
Independent, Glasgow Evening Times, Daily Record,
Scotland on Sunday, The Guardian, The Express, Toronto
Sun, News of the World, London Evening Standard, Mail
on Sunday, The Independent, The Scotsman, The Herald.*

We would like to thank the following photographers,
photographic agencies, film companies and libraries: All
Action; All Action/Foto Blitz/Stills; Jean Cummings/All
Action; Alpha; the British Film Institute; Camera Press;
Lorraine Felix/Camera Press; Capital Pictures; Jerry
Fitzgerald/Corbis/Everett Collection; Tristar/Corbis/Everett
Collection; the Ronald Grant Archive; Kalpesh
Lathigra/The Independent; Moviestore Collection; Kurt
Krieger/MPA; Peter Borsari/Laura Luongo/People in
Picures; Jeff Kravitz/People in Pictures; Polygram Film
International; Bill Davila/ Retna; Steve Granitz/Retna;
Janet Macoska/Retna; Marissa Roth/Retna; John
Spellman/ Retna; Alan Berliner/Liaison/Gamma/Frank
Spooner Agency; Jimmy Gaston/Frank Spooner Agency;
New Line Cinema; Warner Brothers; Paramount Pictures;
Touchstone; Tri Star/JSB Productions; Island Pictures/New
Line Cinema; Capital Films/Fine Line/Fine Line Features;
Cine-Tamaris/France 3 Cinema (FR3)/Recorded Pictures
Company; Tribeca Productions; Bazmark/ 20th Century
Fox; Polygram Film International.

Contents

Introduction

'It's easy to fall into the trap of believing all the hype that's written about you . . . Who knows? In a couple of years, you might find me in the loony bin!'

Leonardo DiCaprio

LEONARDO DICAPRIO has grown up in public. He spent his teenage years in front of movie cameras making a series of critically acclaimed films featuring assured and captivating performances. As he approaches his mid-20s, Leonardo has achieved more than many of Hollywood's biggest movie stars do in entire lifetimes. He's tackled one of the classic romantic roles of stage and screen in *William Shakespeare's Romeo & Juliet*, but set out to make his Romeo a figurehead for 90s youth, an icon of the Ecstasy generation. Leonardo has also won the acclaim of his peers through his nomination for a Best Supporting Actor Oscar for his role as Arnie in *What's Eating Gilbert Grape?*. He was only nineteen.

His rise to stardom in Hollywood is not that surprising – he was born there. Living with his mother in the heart of the movie industry, each day he saw drug abuse and prostitution, rather than glamour, on his way to school. Each night he'd see on TV, or at the movies, the people who did the other kind of work that went on in his hometown district of Los Angeles – movies and movie stars. He dreamt of joining them one day.

Leonardo is worldly wise and grown-up before his years on screen, but off screen he plays the big kid, subjecting his co-stars to practical jokes and inappropriate childish comments. He has worked with some of the greatest talents Hollywood has to offer, among them Robert DeNiro (twice), Meryl Streep, Diane Keaton and Sharon Stone. He even managed to upstage Johnny Depp, a youth icon who'd preceded him, by stealing the acting kudos for *What's Eating Gilbert Grape?* from under Depp's nose.

'I like to be able to play a character and act out a lot of things which I can't or don't do in my normal everyday life.'

Leonardo has done all this from the basest of motivations – he has gleefully admitted that it was the lure of easy money which drew him into acting. It has been all the more surprising to him, to critics and to audiences, that he turned out to be a natural talent, an actor to whom the deepest emotions and most complex portrayals come easily, despite his youth. 'I like to be able to play a character and act out a lot of things which I can't or don't do in my normal everyday life,' he has said. 'It gives me a legal excuse to go nuts with the character. The more nuts I go and the more I show, the deeper I get into the depression or the happiness or the anger of the character, and the more real it is.'

Plunging into an acting career at the early age of five, Leonardo has never stopped to realise what he has become to modern Hollywood – nothing less than one of the most acclaimed actors of his generation. 'I've just been jolting along from one film to another,' he admitted. 'I've never looked back. Now, it's sort of a shock to realise what I've achieved.'

As he wrapped filming on James Cameron's epic romance *Titanic*, probably the most expensive movie ever made, Leonardo took stock of his career, his achievements, and looked to his future. He has enjoyed great success and critical acclaim, carving a career as a less physical, more intellectual or spiritual movie star. Leonardo is not one of Hollywood's beefcake pin-ups – he writes poetry, after all. Although his name had caused him problems early on, the hint of European aristocracy it contains has not

'Don't think for a moment that I'm really like any of the characters I've played. I'm not. That's why it's called "acting".'

harmed his prospects. Leonardo deliberately cultivates an air of mystery, of elusive romance and sophistication beyond his years. At the same time, his restless nature means he has a tendency to be childish and juvenile, a trait which has equally delighted and upset his co-stars. It's been a necessary characteristic, though, as it's a clue to where his seemingly natural ability to incarnate a diverse range of 'outsiders' comes from.

Outsiders and misfits have made up the bulk of his roles, from disaffected youths in *This Boy's Life*, *What's Eating Gilbert Grape?* and *Marvin's Room* to The Kid in *The Quick And The Dead*, Romeo who falls in love across forbidden lines and Jack Dawson in *Titanic*, from the wrong side of the social divide. 'It just seems to be what's most colourful for me,' he has said of these misfit roles, but his acting parts are not really a clue to who he is. 'Don't think for a moment that I'm really like any of the characters I've played. I'm not. That's why it's called "acting".'

Leonardo struck gold in the hip, modern version of William Shakespeare's *Romeo And Juliet*. He was seduced into doing the oft-played role by the director Baz Luhrmann. 'Our *Romeo And Juliet* is a little more hard-core and a lot cooler,' he claimed. It was his breakthough role, the one that propelled Leonardo straight onto the A-list of Hollywood actors. The young boy from the wrong side of the Hollywood tracks had made it to the big time.

Cautious and wary of the fickleness of fame, Leonardo must now take a more serious approach to his long term goals if he is to become a lasting presence on the silver screen. 'One day you're hot, one day you're not,' he has realised. He knows it is time to change, through his roles in *Titanic* and *The Man In The Iron Mask*. He must take on more adult roles, if he is to carve out a lasting career for himself. 'It's easy to fall into the trap of believing all the hype that's written about you,' admitted Leonardo of his good fortune so far. 'I'm trying to avoid it. Who knows? In a couple of years, you might find me in the loony bin!'

His story is that of the typical American teenager, searching for himself, for a definition of who he is as he grows to adulthood. In Leonardo's case, it's been through a series of fictional characters that his search has been pursued. Having lost himself in the people he has played, his biggest fear is that as adulthood beckons, he doesn't know who he really is.

'I've just been jolting along from one film to another . . . Now, it's sort of a shock to realise what I've achieved.'

Growing Pains

'I remember the "Checkered Demon". He's this little devil with this three-foot dong that just porks everybody. And that was my idea of what sex was about. And I was, "Oh, wow! I can't wait."'

Leonardo DiCaprio

L EONARDO WILHELM DICAPRIO was born in Los Angeles on 11th November 1974 to burnt-out hippie parents who named him after the Renaissance artist Leonardo Da Vinci. His mother, German-born Irmelin Idenbirken chose her son's name after feeling him kicking in the womb as she stood in front of a Da Vinci painting in the Uffizi Gallery in Venice, Italy. Even before his birth, Leonardo seemed to have mastered the art of theatrical timing. Leonardo's father, Italian-American George DiCaprio, was delighted with the name, as Leonardo's grandfather on George's side of the family had Leon as a middle name.

When she became pregnant Irmelin, a legal secretary, had been together with George DiCaprio for close to a decade, having met him in college after moving to America from Germany. The pair had spent the sixties exploring the ups and **'My mother is a walking miracle . . .'** downs of the underground counter-culture before marrying and moving, with little money, to Los Angeles. By the time Leonardo had reached his first birthday, his parents had separated, their romance over. 'They didn't want it anymore, I guess,' lamented Leonardo, who was sent on a trip on a Russian cruise ship with Irmelin's parents while his own split their belongings and moved into separate households, promising to stay friends if only for Leonardo's sake.

Leonardo grew up under the watchful eye of his mother in a poor area of Hollywood. Nevertheless, he continued to spend a great deal of time with his father as his parents remained close after their separation. 'George and I have always spent a lot of time together with Leonardo,' confirmed Irmelin. 'While he was growing up we always had dinner together and took him out to amusement parks and movies.' Leonardo maintained that his parents' separation did not have a strong effect on him growing up, such was the continued presence in his life of his father. Indeed, as his film career developed, his mother handled his business affairs, while his father helped Leonardo filter through the many scripts he received. His parents' partnership continued, not as an emotional union but as a business venture based on Leonardo's growing acting career.

'My mother is a walking miracle . . . She was in World War Two in Germany and

'My dad has always been the bohemian . . .'

Far left: Leonardo, as he was when he won the role of Gary Buckman on the short-lived Parenthood TV series. Left: 'I insist on keeping level headed,' said Leonardo of his response to fame and fortune.

she had so many brushes with death,' said Leonardo. 'My mother is cool. She really doesn't care about this whole thing [fame] – she truly doesn't. She separates herself from it. She's the only one who genuinely cares for what I do as a person, and doesn't make my career out to be more than a job, which is what it is. If I worked a nine-to-five office job, she'd feel the same way and have the same enthusiasm.'

As his maternal grandparents were still living in Germany, Leonardo had visited the country over half a dozen times before his tenth birthday. He travelled with Irmelin to see 'Oma' and 'Opa', as he called his grandma and grandpa in his earliest German-language

'My dad's probably one of the kindest people in the world. When I was younger that's not how I was – I was a little spoiled brat.'

baby talk. Irmelin wasted no time in teaching her son German, and by his teens Leonardo was as fluent as she was. Leonardo was close to his German grandparents, visiting Düsseldorf's flea markets with them, or walking in the forest near their home with his grandfather, who would tell him stories of the past. 'I love my grandfather because he is lots of fun to be with,' Leonardo once told an interviewer. 'I really enjoy talking with him because he always makes me laugh. He loves to joke around with me, and he cracks me up.' Leonardo inherited his love of jokes and practical pranks which would often infuriate his movie co-stars from his grandfather. His grandfather's serious illness and subsequent death during the making of *Total Eclipse*, later in Leonardo's film career, was one factor that made working on that film in France so difficult for him.

Back in the United States, his father took Leonardo out on many trips at weekends, often visiting a museum or comic book store. Alternatively, they might spend a Saturday afternoon scouring through boxes full of old baseball cards, looking for the rare cards Leonardo needed to complete his collection. 'My dad has always been there for me,' said Leonardo. 'I've never missed out on the so-called normal father-son relationship because I saw him anytime I wanted. We always had a lot of fun together.'

'I don't think my parents would be shocked about anything I did, because they're so laid-back.'

Leonardo's father had been a significant figure in the world of sixties alternative literature and underground comics. Leonardo grew up around such luminaries of the period as cartoonist Robert Crumb and writer Hubert Selby Jnr, who gave the new-born Leonardo a tiny set of boxing gloves as a gift. 'My dad told me how important they were,' recalled Leonardo, who remembered being singularly unimpressed by his father's famous friends. 'I didn't really care.'

George had been in New York for much of the sixties, rooming with Velvet Underground guitarist Sterling Morrison and publishing a comic book, *Baloney Moccasins*, with his one-time girlfriend, performance artist Laurie Anderson. He moved to Los Angeles with Irmelin in the early seventies and continued to distribute underground comics and beatnik books to local bookstores, as well as arranging public readings for the likes of William Burroughs and Allen Ginsberg. America Hoffman, son of sixties radical Abbie Hoffman, was one of Leonardo's closest childhood friends.

'My dad has always been the bohemian,' confirmed Leonardo. 'He's still doing it, as far as how he lives his life, as far as his views on the Government. He's got the long hair and the beard. He knows the underground artist scene, he's been into comic art for a long time. I definitely have gotten a lot of values from that. My dad's probably one of the kindest people in the world. When I was younger that's not how I was – I was a little spoiled brat.'

Coming from an unconventional background, Leonardo enjoyed trying to prove that he was just an ordinary kid, not that different from anyone else. 'We're not the hippie family that everyone imagines – the children don't meditate and we eat things other than organic foods. But then, we're not exactly the normal run-of-the-mill family you get living next door, either.'

His parents' tolerance for his childhood antics and their lack of discipline and controls would prove to be both a blessing and a curse for Leonardo. 'I don't think my parents would be shocked about anything I did, because they're so laid-back,' he admitted. Leonardo had no firm rules to rebel against, which allowed him great freedom and may have been instrumental in him developing the acting talents he would later display, but it also resulted in a lack of maturity as he got older and a constant desire to 'play the big kid'.

While laying claim to a fairly normal childhood, Leonardo is also full of stories of how dreadful his life was growing up poor with a single mother in a notoriously dangerous area of Hollywood Boulevard, known as Syringe Alley. 'We were in the poorhouse. I would walk to my playground and see, like, a guy open up his trench coat with a thousand syringes. If you went there right now it would be filled with prostitutes and drug addicts on the streets. It was a bit of a shock. I lived in the ghettos of Hollywood, right near the old Hollywood Billiards – it was the most disgusting place to be. My mom, who thought Hollywood was the place where all the great stuff was going on, took great care of me, but I was able to see all sorts of stuff at an early age.' Irmelin and Leonardo later moved to a house in the Los Feliz area of Los Angeles, where he lived with her until the age of twenty in 1994, when he finally moved to a home of his own, several years after his movie career had begun.

Leonardo was a wilful youngster, making it difficult for his mother to place him in day-care during his pre-school days. He recalls being driven by Irmelin to visit his new pre-school in an outer area of Los Angeles. 'That's where you're going to be in two weeks,' she told Leonardo. He remembers starting to cry, wailing, 'Am I going to stay all the way out here all day? Nooo, I wanna stay home!' Irmelin ended up solving her childcare worries by becoming a childminder for the neighbourhood kids, and keeping Leonardo at home.

One of Leonardo's main childhood interests was animals and pets of all kinds. Unfortunately, his relationships with animals seemed more often than not to end up in the poor creature's death. Leonardo vividly recalls the day his pet cat, named Germain, died in a fight with another cat, and his mother's then boyfriend threw the corpse in the garbage. Animals became a passion for him, to the extent that he brought home a

Leonardo won a high profile role in the sit com Growing Pains *in 1991, co-starring with Alan Thicke and Kirk Cameron.*

group of frogs from the swamp one day and kept them in a cage. When he was cleaning the cage, Leonardo popped the frogs into a bowl and covered it with clingfilm to prevent their escape. It wasn't a good move. 'It was like a condensed microwave for them, and when I came back, they were all burned and in different contorted positions. I'll never forget that. I cried about that.' Later, Leonardo took over the care of an epileptic dog named Rocky the Rottweiler who was on his last legs before Leonardo came along. He researched canine epilepsy and managed to suggest a new drug regime for his pooch. 'My dog Rocky is probably one of the most unfortunate hounds in the world. He was the runt of the litter, got stolen and was almost sold to the black market when he was two. He has constant seizures, and he's on medication, so he's tired all the time. He was overweight before the medication, and now we've just found out he has cancer. My mom treats him like a new-born child, so he's happy.'

There were other animal misfortunes in Leonardo's early days. 'I remember vividly – for some reason this has been in my thoughts – killing a pigeon. The pigeon was limping and my friend had a gun, so we decided to shoot it to put it out of its misery. And it wouldn't die, so we had to shoot it at least 10 or 15 more times, and it was this gruelling torture of the goddamned pigeon. And I was sitting there, and I was crying, looking at this pigeon who just kept getting shot in the head and the back, and who just kept wobbling. And finally my stepbrother just took a board and went crkkkk! and killed it.'

'What I really wanted was to travel and see all the different animals that were on the verge of extinction.'

Despite his animal antics and his parents' counter-culture interests and lifestyle, Leonardo did enjoy a relatively normal childhood packed with ordinary childhood pursuits. He was deeply interested in the sea as a youngster, wanting to be an oceanographer when he grew up. One of his heroes was Poseidon, Greek god of the sea, and Leonardo would proudly display the scar on his upper right arm caused when he got too friendly with a Portuguese man 'o war. Tropical islands and the underwater themed cartoon TV show *Submariner* were also big youthful passions. His favourite film as a child was *King Kong*. Later this was replaced in his affections by Tod Browning's controversial *Freaks* and Francis Ford Coppola's *Godfather* trilogy, which featured his favourite actors – Al Pacino and Robert DeNiro. He also liked *Star Wars* and had a favourite character: 'It's Chewbacca. I was real young when I first saw the movie, but I was fascinated by him. I also had my own little Ewok village to play with.' Stevie Wonder was young Leonardo's unlikely choice as his favourite musician during his childhood days.

He had other vague career ambitions, along the lines of being a businessman, a lawyer or even a travel agent. He saw travel as a way to combine both his interest in the sea and his keenness for animals. 'What I really wanted was to travel and see all the different animals that were on the verge of extinction,' he said much later looking back at his childhood ambitions. 'I still want to go and see a bunch of animals in Madagascar, and the Galapagos islands and stuff. And I've researched all the ones that are already extinct. It really makes me sad.' Later he would make generous donations to a fund aimed at saving the Manatees in Florida from extinction.

Despite this normality, Leonardo's humble beginnings in a bullet-ridden area of Los Angeles stayed with him for many years. One traumatic experience in particular had a strong effect on him. 'I saw some major homosexual activity outside my friend's balcony when I was five. To this day it's an imprint on my mind,' he recalled, giving a clue to some of the difficulties he would face later while playing homosexual scenes during the making of the movie *Total Eclipse* with David Thewlis.

At school, the young Leonardo would do anything to avoid expanding his mind. He was educated at the Centre for Enriched Studies and the John Marshall High School, both in Los Angeles. Education and learning did not appeal to him and he often cheated to get through classes, especially in maths. His restless nature limited his concentration. 'I never truly got the knack of what school was all about. I was unable to focus or concentrate on anything. I wasn't interested in learning – it made some classes a bit tricky. I was more interested in break-dancing with my pals in front of the other pupils at lunchtime. I was always the kid in school who tried to get attention, not necessarily the class clown, but I'd do little unexpected performances.' A favourite impression for Leonardo to perform was of singer Michael Jackson and he could do a mean moonwalk. He'd still be doing it years later to entertain the cast and crew when shooting in Mexico on *William Shakespeare's Romeo & Juliet*.

He wasn't the kind of kid who got into serious trouble at school, but Leonardo does recall shoplifting bubblegum from a grocery store and later, at the age of nine, he was seriously told off for drawing a swastika on his forehead and imitating Charles Manson. It was a further example of lack of parental control for Leonardo to rebel against. 'I didn't know who he was at the time or what he did,' claimed Leonardo of the Manson incident. 'I went to school with this swastika on my forehead and started talking about biting dogs heads off and I really had no idea what I was talking about. I was sent home from school and had no idea that I was doing anything wrong. That was the sick part of it – when you're young you do stuff like that.' Leonardo failed to graduate, dropping out of school with no clear career prospects. His education was only really re-established when he won a series of TV roles, resulting in the legal requirement for him to have a private tutor when not working on set.

'I was always the kid in school who tried to get attention, not necessarily the class clown, but I'd do little unexpected performances.'

There was one area of learning which did pique the interest of the pre-adolescent Leonardo: sex. When he was six, Leonardo's father suggested his son should lose his virginity. The pair were sitting in a car when his father suddenly announced: 'The first time I had sex I was your age. You should try it.' According to Leonardo, he wasn't interested, telling his father: 'Shut up dad, I don't want to try it. I'm gonna do all my homework instead.' The only way for Leonardo to rebel against the wide-ranging freedoms he was given by his parents was to refuse them. 'He used to show me all these weird magazines,' said Leonardo of his father's collection of underground literature, stored up in his garage. 'I used to run in and look at all the dirty underground sex magazines when I was younger – comic book sex.'

This unconventional introduction to the topic was to give the young Leonardo some bizarre ideas of what sex was all about. 'I remember the "Checkered Demon". He's this little devil with this three-foot dong that just porks everybody. And that was my idea of what sex was about. And I was, "Oh, wow! I can't wait".'

Bored at school by the actual classes, Leonardo would pass the time by studying the girls. 'There was this one girl in elementary school who would just stay there and watch the chickens all day in this little chicken coop. And all I would do every day is watch her without her seeing me. It was the weirdest thing. I would just stand behind a tree – just admiring her. She was tall, she had black hair and big eyes. I never spoke to her.'

As he grew up, Leonardo worked on his chat-up technique, determined to get past that first hurdle of actually starting a conversation. 'I was about sixteen when I learnt how to flirt and I had a bit of a routine going on.'

Playing to audiences was something Leonardo discovered he had a knack for at an early age. He recalls being taken by his father to a performance festival – 'I had my red jumpsuit on and my tackiest shirt' – and his father suggesting, 'Hey, go up on stage.' Leonardo did just that and found himself looking out at a sea of expectant faces. Overcoming a moment's hesitation, the youngster began to dance. 'Tappity, tappity, tappity,' remembered Leonardo. 'They were like, "Yeah – more". There's me getting more attention, me! There was no stopping me and my dad had to pull me off the stage.'

Although he didn't rush off to join the circus, take to the stage or start making movies right away, Leonardo had a strong feeling early in his childhood that acting might be something he could do. 'I was always waiting for something,' recalled Leonardo of his childhood days. 'I always had this feeling. That's the truth, not some nice little fairy tale. I didn't know whether it was going to be in acting or whatever, but I was going to get lucky. I didn't even plan for college because I was determined that it was going to happen.'

'I was about sixteen when I learnt how to flirt and I had a bit of a routine going on.'

Leonardo made his screen debut on television at the tender age of five in the children's TV show *Romper Room*. This was something of a false start in showbusiness for the youngster as he was thrown off the set for his 'uncontrollable behaviour'. It would be over ten years before he secured his first big screen role and a few more years after that before he was to make it big in Hollywood.

Showbusiness success began to happen first not for Leonardo but for his step-brother, Adam Starr. Leonardo's father, George, had remarried and was raising his second wife's son. Adam was signed, through connections made by George DiCaprio, to appear in a Golden Grahams breakfast cereal commercial. 'I asked my dad how much Adam made from it,' remembers Leonardo of his initial motivation for pursuing an acting career. 'He said, "About $50,000." Fifty thousand dollars! It just kept going through my head: My brother has $50,000 dollars! And that kept on being my driving force. I just remember for, like, five years thinking my brother was better than me because he had that.'

Leonardo's next steps in the world of acting came at the age of fourteen when he signed with an agent and featured in over two dozen television commercials (including one for Matchbox cars, bubblegum, breakfast cereals and other toys) and short educational films. The money his brother had gained from just one commercial was the driving force for the young Leonardo. He never took any theatre classes or signed up for any formal acting training – the thought didn't even cross his mind. He just kept the financial possibilities in front of him as he attended audition after audition, being rejected at many for sometimes bizarre reasons, like having the 'wrong haircut'. He recalls returning home with his father after another audition where he'd suffered yet another humiliating rejection. He said: 'Dad, I really want to become an actor, but if this is what it's all about, I don't want to do it.' It was George DiCaprio's wise words of patience that kept Leonardo persevering with his attempts: 'Someday, Leonardo, it will happen for you. Remember these words – just relax.' It was typical of the laid-back attitude that Leonardo's father had to all aspects of life.

To secure parts, Leonardo even tried out for a while under a stage name. He was determined to keep it a secret later in life, but it appears that one prospective agent

'Dad, I really want to become an actor, but if this is what it's all about, I don't want to do it.'

'That movie made me understand what I was really good at,' said Leonardo of his breakthrough role in This Boy's Life.

asked him to change his name to Lenny Williams. It was hoped he would be able to secure more parts with a more 'ordinary', less 'ethnic' name. The same problem had been faced by Keanu Reeves in his early days. The attempt to change Leonardo's name was short lived. When he failed to win any more parts as Lenny Williams, the new name was consigned to history and he changed back to Leonardo DiCaprio. Despite doubts about the suitability of his name, Leonardo was getting some work, even if it was only the odd commercial or short information film. It all kept him busy – and the lure of big financial rewards kept Leonardo attending soul-destroying auditions.

Suddenly, Leonardo's acting opportunities began to eclipse those of his step-brother Adam. Adam Starr had gone on to feature in further commercials and won a regular role

in the late 70s TV space series *Battlestar Galactica*, but later gave up on acting in order to join the army. Leonardo was signed up by a talent agent who knew a friend of his mother, and his acting career began in earnest. For Leonardo work seemed to generate more work and opportunities multiplied the more he pursued them. In the two years between the ages of fourteen to sixteen, Leonardo made about twenty TV commercials. Educational films were also a large part of Leonardo's early work, including a never-screened public service announcement on the dangers of drugs in which a crack vial in Leonardo's mouth turned into a shotgun. 'Don't cross the street without looking both ways,' announced fifteen-year-old Leonardo in a short film made for the Disney TV show *Mickey's Safety Club*. He featured in another public service announcement, this time entitled *How To Deal With A Parent Who Takes Drugs*. 'It was not exactly a career booster,' he later admitted.

Next thing he knew, he began to win guest roles in various TV series, starting with a two part tale in *Lassie*. 'Lassie was having puppies before the big BMX bike race and I was the sort of young cocky kid who just wanted to win . . . ,' said Leonardo of starring alongside Hollywood's best known – and longest lived – dog. He also made a brief guest appearance in a TV show called *A Circus Fantasy* and featured in episodes of popular sitcom *Roseanne*.

He then popped up in *The Outsiders*, a short lived show based on the 'brat pack' movie directed by Francis Ford Coppola, and joined the regular cast of daytime soap *Santa Barbara* playing the challenging role of a

Following This Boy's
Life, *Leonardo's
Hollywood prospects
opened up.*

teenage alcoholic. The daily grind of production on a soap was something of a shock
for the fifteen-year-old. Due to his age and working restrictions he was only allowed
to be on the set for half the working day, but he still had huge amounts of dialogue to
prepare before the live taping that these shows adopted. On top of that his character
had to go through a series of emotionally gruelling scenes. Despite the slog, it was a
useful acting apprenticeship.

Better than the soap opera
role – which was not what
Leonardo wanted to do with

'Portraying emotionally ill characters gives me the chance to really act.'

his blossoming acting career – was securing a featured part as Garry Buckman in the TV
sitcom spin-off from the 1989 hit movie *Parenthood*. This was a high profile, prime-time
show, and a chance for Leonardo to be seen every week, Saturday nights at 8pm on
NBC. The run started on 20th August 1990 and featured Leonardo among a regular
ensemble cast of fifteen. Again, as in his film work to come, Leonardo played the
troubled teen. 'I haven't portrayed a cheerful boy yet,' he once said, somewhat gleefully.
'Portraying emotionally ill characters gives me the chance to really act.' Unfortunately,
Parenthood was not the hit the network had hoped for and it was off the air by
December 1990, after just a few months. Just as he was getting used to regular series
work, Leonardo was out of a job.

Leonardo's biggest break yet came on the TV series *Growing Pains* in 1991, at the
age of seventeen. The schmaltzy sitcom had, since 1985, been a vehicle for eighties teen
TV star Kirk Cameron, who was now considered by the show's producers to be too old
for the programme's audience: 'That was when I was sent on, to rekindle the young

girls' lust for a young man.' Leonardo played the part of a young homeless boy named Luke Brower, making frequent regular appearances on the show during its final season on air. His character moved in with the family, the Seavers, featured in the series for 24 episodes and served to highlight some of the issues surrounding the young homeless in America, something Leonardo was keen to talk about in teen magazine interviews promoting the show. He wasn't the saviour for the series that the producers hoped, and the show was later cancelled. 'The new writing was awful,' claimed Leonardo. 'Either that or I'm not sexy at all. Either one – you tell me.' Despite the possibility that Leonardo's character might get picked up for his own series, time was running out for *Growing Pains* as the ratings continued to fall. The seventh year was its last, and Leonardo faced the prospect of losing a role once again.

The exposure on the show did serve to raise Leonardo's profile, with features beginning to appear on the young actor in the teen fan magazines. Photoshoots promoting *Parenthood* and *Growing Pains* often focused on Leonardo at the expense of other cast members. Leonardo stood out from many of the others, sometimes due to his fooling around rather than simply for his clean-cut good looks. Irmelin became involved in co-ordinating her son's publicity, resulting in coverage for him in many teen magazines, like the ever-popular *Dream Guy*. Her Faustian pact with the press was to rebound on her and Leonardo later in his career, but for the moment, the increased exposure suited them both.

'I've been planted here to be a vessel for acting ...' That's why I'm really taking any part, regardless of how complicated it's going to be ...'

The primary benefit that Leonardo drew from his days on *Growing Pains* was an awareness of what he didn't want to do as an actor: 'I had these lame lines. I couldn't bear it actually. Everyone was bright and chipper.' Although his TV stardom was minor and short lived, it was to be a taste of things to come as Leonardo switched his energies to big screen movie roles.

As far as film debuts go, Leonardo's first film acting experience at the age of sixteen was an inauspicious start to a dramatic and fast-moving career. His big screen debut came in the unlikely form of the 1991 movie *Critters 3*, in which he battled tiny furball invaders and dodgy dialogue with similar panache. He made the film – the latest in a line of bad B-movie sequels to the 1986 *Gremlins* knockoff, *Critters* – just before winning the regular role on *Growing Pains*.

'You found out about that one, huh,' said Leonardo of his Z-grade movie debut. 'It was possibly one of the worst films of all time. I guess it was a good example to look back on and make sure it doesn't happen again.' Following earlier suggestions from agents that he make his name more appealing, he was billed as 'Leonard' in the credits of *Critters 3*. To this day, Leonardo prefers to have his co-starring role with Robert DeNiro in *This Boy's Life* noted as his cinematic debut, even though it was actually his third feature film. In a sense Leonardo's claim is partially true, as *Critters 3* was so poor it bypassed cinemas altogether, going straight to video release instead.

Leonardo's first line in the film was 'Hey! Don't go down there, kid. There's all kinds of weird animals and shit.' It was not the kind of material to bring the young actor any attention at this stage from those who award the annual Oscars. The plot of *Critters 3* concerned the residents of a run down Los Angeles apartment block who are driven onto the roof of the building by hoards of the hairy, toothsome creatures. 'My most brilliant performance,' joked Leonardo about his debut effort. 'Those are the kind of films I want to do more of,' he added ironically. Although hardly memorable material, the third in the *Critters* series of films was slightly better than its predecessors. Leonard Maltin in his *Movie and Video Guide* described the film as having 'not quite enough Critters action . . . but with better characters than usual.'

'I really don't know what I'm doing . . . I don't. It's terrible. I go in there and I learn how to be like the character and do the best I can, and that's all I really do.'

His first priority – as the role in *Critters 3* showed – was not to be too choosy about the roles he accepted, just to keep working and to make the move from TV to feature films. 'I've been planted here to be a vessel for acting,' he once claimed, rather pretentiously. 'That's why I'm really taking any part, regardless of how complicated it's going to be, because I'd feel selfish otherwise. It's like cheating. It's hard to explain.' It was an attitude that Leonardo was to change as his career developed, his parts got better and he didn't feel the need to accept any role offered.

His next blink-and-you'll-miss-him role was in the thriller *Poison Ivy*, a comeback film for Drew Barrymore, the then seventeen-year-old one-time child star (in *ET: The Extra Terrestrial*, among others) and celebrity. Drawing much from the films of Alfred Hitchcock, Katt Shea Ruben's smart and witty genre thriller cast Barrymore as Ivy. She has a malign influence on a family which seems on the verge of falling apart anyway, with a mischievous daughter (Sara Gilbert, from TV's *Roseanne*), her dying, drug addled mom (Cheryl Ladd) and alcoholic right-wing TV-pundit dad (Tom Skerrit). Leonardo appears fleetingly in the opening sequence as the denim-clad member of a teenage gang who discovers a dog run over by a car. The dog's still breathing, but is quickly put out of its misery by Ivy and an iron bar. His character is billed in the credits as 'Guy', but he is never identified in the film. It was little more than a bit part with none of his dialogue left in the movie – but he did get a chance to hook up again with Sara Gilbert whom he'd met when guest starring on *Roseanne*.

It's clear that while Leonardo felt he could make a living from acting, he was also concerned to pay his dues in the film world by learning some of the craft to supplement his blossoming natural talent. From his prominent TV roles in *Parenthood* and *Growing Pains*, Leonardo had made the switch to movie acting, even though it was in poor material like *Critters 3* and *Poison Ivy*. It had all been a useful apprenticeship for the actor who was about to get the chance to show just what he could do, starring alongside Robert DeNiro in *This Boy's Life*. Despite his increasing success and evident talent, Leonardo himself was mystified by the source of his acting abilities: 'I really don't know what I'm doing,' said Leonardo of his early screen outings. 'I don't. It's terrible. I go in there and I learn how to be like the character and do the best I can, and that's all I really do.'

Leo Rising

'My career should adapt to me. Fame is like a VIP pass wherever you want to go.'
Leonardo DiCaprio

FOLLOWING HIS BATTLES with the furry invaders in *Critters 3* and dealing with the melodrama of *Poison Ivy*, Leonardo DiCaprio's big cinematic breakthrough came when he co-starred with Hollywood veterans Robert DeNiro and Ellen Barkin in Michael Caton-Jones' emotional true-life drama *This Boy's Life*, made in 1993.

Scottish born director Michael Caton-Jones had enjoyed a high profile directorial debut with *Scandal*, the retelling of the British Profumo political scandal of the sixties, starring John Hurt and Bridget Fonda. The critical and popular success of the film allowed Caton-Jones to tackle a personal project, the World War Two drama *Memphis Belle*, before directing another popular hit comedy, the Michael J. Fox vehicle *Doc Hollywood*.

Based on the autobiography of author Tobias Wolff, published in 1989, *This Boy's Life* tells an often harrowing tale of adolescence as Toby Wolff (Leonardo) survives his abusive relationship with his stepfather, played by Robert DeNiro. Producer Art Linson summed the film up as 'a wonderful memoir of growing up – a true story of a boy overcoming some tough situations. What no one would have expected from Toby Wolff was that, given his background, he would become an English professor and prominent writer.'

Said Caton-Jones of his cast: 'I have three excellent actors in this film, but Leonardo is the rock that this movie is built on. If people can't relate to the character of Toby, the story becomes voyeuristic, but Leonardo makes this kid's struggle something you can connect with immediately.'

The weight of the film rested on the shoulders of Leonardo. He'd secured the part after a series of gruelling interviews and auditions, beating over 400 other hopefuls to the role after a four-month casting search which ranged from Los Angeles to New York and Florida and all points in between, as Caton-Jones searched for the perfect actor to portray Toby. Leonardo had been one of the first actors to read for the part, but director Caton-Jones was wary of deciding so early in the process. 'It was simple – I knew he was it, but when someone reads for you that early, you don't believe it. So we tried loads and loads of young actors, but we came right back to Leonardo,' he confirmed.

Playing Tobias Wolff, Leonardo had to read up on life in the late fifties, as well as adopting the right look.

Leonardo beat over 400 hopefuls to star with Ellen Barkin and Robert DeNiro in This Boy's Life.

Part of this exhaustive auditioning process involved a script-reading session for shortlisted actors with Robert DeNiro, who the teenage Leonardo considered a Hollywood legend. The young actor's youthful bravado was enough to carry him through the encounter which might have had some others stuttering and stumbling over their lines, awed by DeNiro's presence. 'I didn't worry about what DeNiro thought,' claimed Leonardo. 'I went in, looked him in the eye and got the part. I was confident, even though I'd never done anything like it before. Now I realise it was ignorant confidence – I had no idea.'

Producer Art Linson felt they were lucky to find Leonardo, believing him to be an actor who could carry the weight of making the central, youthful character believable. 'This movie is about someone growing up and dealing with a mother he's very close to and a stepfather he's trying to get away from. Toby's situation makes for a fascinating story, but it's also a metaphor for all the teenagers who feel similar in less desperate circumstances. Leonardo makes that possible with his performance.'

Leonardo was grateful to DeNiro for taking time out from concentrating on his own performance in the film to guide the youngster in some of the finer points of screen acting. These tutorials helped Leonardo deliver a more polished final performance than Caton-Jones ever expected from his new discovery. 'It was cool, very cool,' said Leonardo of DeNiro's guidance and example-setting performance. 'He was very free when he rehearsed it and very creative, but much more business-like when he went in there for a take.'

Leonardo's adult approach to winning the role in *This Boy's Life* and working with DeNiro was something else which came naturally to him. 'Earlier, at fourteen I

> **'I didn't worry about what DeNiro thought . . . I went in, looked him in the eye and got the part. I was confident, even though I'd never done anything like it before. Now I realise it was ignorant confidence – I had no idea.'**

was already wanting to be recognised as an adult; when I was doing *This Boy's Life* I wanted to be as old as Robert DeNiro and as experienced as him and have the same respect as he did in that movie. I'm just starting to scratch the surface of what really makes me happy,' said Leonardo.

To play the part, Leonardo had to get under the skin of Tobias Wolff. That the story was true helped the young actor to bring his character to life. 'This role was different from any other I had played,' recalled Leonardo. 'This was something that was true, that actually happened to this guy. When you are in the moment of a powerful story like that, you just can't help but feel emotionally disrupted.'

Leonardo's restlessness, which had affected his schooling, contributed in a different way to his work. He found himself able to play things in an adult manner, impressing DeNiro and Caton-Jones, but he was also to develop a liking for practical jokes and larking around on the set, which led his *William Shakespeare's Romeo & Juliet* co-star Claire Danes to label him 'somewhat immature'.

'. . . when I was doing *This Boy's Life* I wanted to be as old as Robert DeNiro and as experienced as him and have the same respect as he did in that movie.'

For *This Boy's Life* Leonardo travelled to Vancouver, British Columbia, where, in the forested hills above the city, principal photography on the film was to take place on a single primary set, Dwight Hansen's shabby rural house. Later the company travelled to Moab and Salt Lake City in Utah, as well as to Concrete, Washington – the small Cascade Mountain town, 100 miles north-east of Seattle, where author Tobias Wolff grew up. Considerable work was required to return the small town to the look it had in the late fifties, when the movie is set. Ten days were spent shooting there, but weeks of renovation and alteration took place beforehand in preparation.

Considering his limited acting experience and the fact that he'd not tackled heavy dramatic roles, the part of Toby was always going to be a difficult stretch for Leonardo. However, with Caton-Jones directing and Robert DeNiro advising and guiding the newcomer, Leonardo turned in the first significant performance of his career. Working on the film gave him some insights into his own emerging natural talents and abilities.

'That movie made me understand that this was what I was really good at,' recalled Leonardo of the dawning realisation that there was more to this acting lark than his initial motivation of simply earning plenty of money. To his surprise, he found he actually had some aptitude for bringing complicated characters to life. Leonardo was displaying the kind of acting abilities which escape most young actors his age, but the seemingly faultless performance on screen didn't come too easy to the young actor. 'Michael Caton-Jones said "This ain't happy faces and funny lines – this is the real thing and you'd better work your butt off".'

One thing Leonardo had a problem with early in his career was watching his own performances on screen. 'Most of the time all I can do is look at the negative stuff,' he later said. 'I talked to Michael Caton-Jones after *This Boy's Life* and he told me it takes a couple of years for you to actually appreciate the films you've been in, what you've done, and how you hear people say good or bad things about it. It takes a couple of years for you to realise for yourself what it really is. I'm probably just at that point now where I can appreciate the first movie that I did. The recent ones I can't even look at.'

The eighteen-year-old Leonardo reacts to the onslaught from Robert DeNiro with quiet rebellion.

When it was released in the United States in 1993, *This Boy's Life* grossed only in the region of $4–5 million. Although not a big earner at the box office, the film brought a positive critical reaction, a lot of it centering on Leonardo himself. The film had done its job as far as Hollywood casting agents were concerned – Leonardo DiCaprio was now a name on everyone's lips as a young talent to watch.

'If I want to go to a party with a few male friends, it doesn't mean I'm gay . . .'

One of the scenes in *This Boy's Life* was to do much to define Leonardo's on-screen image and was to fuel much speculation about the young man's off screen life. As Toby, Leonardo gets his first on screen kiss – and it's with another boy. In the scene, after previously tormenting the boy, Leonardo's Toby finds himself sitting at the piano with him, singing show tunes, when they kiss. Michael Caton-Jones called Leonardo 'a really brave actor' for his willingness to tackle the difficult scene.

The door was opened for media speculation on Leonardo's own sexuality, backed up by his later performances in *The Basketball Diaries* and *Total Eclipse*. 'If I want to go to a party with a few male friends, it doesn't mean I'm gay,' said Leonardo later in response to the growing speculation. 'I don't see why I can't have friends of both sexes

without wild rumours being circulated. It's crazy.' His nervousness about playing homosexual roles on screen was to lead to accusations of homophobia, especially when it came to Leonardo's vocal objections during the shooting of *Total Eclipse*.

Rumours like these in the press seemed to affect Leonardo considerably. When asked what were the worst he'd heard, he replied: 'That I'm gay. I heard that I was going out with Ellen Barkin. That I'm an alien. Nothing that odd, I guess.'

It was a small taste of things to come for the actor. *This Boy's Life* gave him a firm grounding in Hollywood and brought him to the attention of casting directors searching for new, young talent. He even secured his first award: the New Generation Award from the Los Angeles Film Critics Association. Michael Caton-Jones speculated on Leonardo's future: 'He'll do intelligent material, with depth, feeling and range, but he'll also have a lot of sex appeal. That's what separates movie stars from everyday actors.' The acclaim didn't make Leonardo an overnight teenage icon. That came slowly, over the next couple of years, but he was philosophical about his start in the movie business. 'You get started with whatever is available and you stick with it until somebody realises, "Hey, this kid can act!"'

'. . . I don't see why I can't have friends of both sexes without wild rumours being circulated. It's crazy.'

Taking a role playing second fiddle to Johnny Depp in *What's Eating Gilbert Grape?*, Leonardo DiCaprio showed he had learned more than mere screen presence from his work opposite Robert DeNiro. Deep research into his character – an eighteen-year-old autistic boy named Arnie – was to take up much of Leonardo's time before filming began on the project. It was to be the only role for which he would indulge DeNiro's method-style approach.

What's Eating Gilbert Grape? was directed by Swedish film-maker Lasse Hallstrom from a novel by Peter Hedges. The novel had only been published for a few days when Hallstrom, known for his Oscar-winning work *My Life as a Dog*, called Hedges to secure the film rights. 'This was great news for me,' recalled Hedges, 'because *My Life as a Dog* is one of my favourite films. I realised that Lasse could bring great humanity to these characters where another director might make fun of them.'

Hedges was drafted to write the screenplay: 'Gilbert Grape (Johhny Depp) is stuck in Endora, working in a grocery story. Everybody's gnawing at him: his family, his brother (Leonardo), his friends, his lover. Into town rolls a girl (Juliette Lewis) who collides with everything that's been closed up inside him.'

For Leonardo, winning the role had not come easy. Even with the acclaim he'd enjoyed for *This Boy's Life*, he was still having to audition, along with every other young actor in Los Angeles, for any likely parts. The process of attending multiple auditions for a single role was gruelling: 'It was one of the hardest things I've ever done.'

'I needed someone who wasn't good looking,' noted Hallstrom of his difficulties in casting the role of Depp's retarded younger brother. 'But of all the actors who auditioned for the role of Arnie, Leonardo was the most observant.'

After several sessions with large numbers of actors, Hallstrom had narrowed things down to a final group he wanted to consider further. To help him make his final choice, he set the actors who'd made it this far a specific task. 'Lasse gave the final group of actors the same tape of a retarded boy,' remembered Leonardo. 'I watched this kid move his eyes and body and just tried to get into his mind. It was interesting because he was completely unpredictable, so I could improvise pretty much whenever

I felt it was right during the scene. I could cry out or burp or yell, whatever. I took a lot of his mannerisms and made them more like my own. I developed the character even more by adding the mannerisms of the other people I had met.'

'I thought the character Lasse chose was way too subdued and internal,' said Leonardo of his first foray into the depths of method acting. 'I went and researched a bunch of other kids. I went to homes. I really wanted to get that feeling of a four-year-old child, a baby almost, with the whole world open to him, rather than the depressing sort of retarded character that you feel sorry for. When I first started I was trying to process all of the information – the various twitches, certain ways of moving, facial expressions. I realised there were many different ways to do this role, thousands of different things I could do.'

During his days visiting homes for the mentally disabled, Leonardo spent time trying to get into the damaged minds of the patients. 'We just talked,' said Leonardo of his visits, 'and I watched their mannerisms and stuff like that. People have these expectations that mentally-retarded children are really crazy, but it's not so. It's refreshing to see them because everything's new to them. They are completely spontaneous and focus on what is directly in their vision, what they experience at that moment. Playing Arnie was fun because everything I did was spontaneous.'

That spontaneity came across on screen. Whether Arnie was clambering up the town's water tower or killing bugs for kicks, the vigorous joy the actor brought to the part came across loud and clear. It was a performance that dominated a film supposedly about the relationship between the Johnny Depp and Juliette Lewis characters. In playing such a strong character and doing it so well and so utterly convincingly, Leonardo stole the movie – a fact later marked by an Oscar nomination.

'Playing Arnie was fun because everything I did was spontaneous.'

Director Lasse Hallstrom was impressed with his young star's emerging talents. 'It comes very easy to him,' he said. 'My only theory is that he has a connection to the four-year-old inside.' It seemed Leonardo's restless energy was being put to good use. His facility to act like a big kid allowed him to convincingly portray so many grown-up misfits, from Arnie Grape to Jim Carroll, Arthur Rimbaud and even Shakespeare's Romeo.

Leonardo's childhood animal obsessions came back to haunt him on the set of *What's Eating Gilbert Grape?* when he fell foul of the on-set animal welfare officers. In an early scene in the film, Leonardo's Arnie places a grasshopper in a mailbox, then slams it shut, decapitating the insect. 'I didn't know I wasn't supposed to kill him. They said put the head in and slam it. So I killed one and that is the take they used. There was a whole bunch of animal rights people on the set to make sure that the fucking grasshopper didn't get its head chopped off, and I didn't know, and they complained. But it was too late when its head was writhing on the floor. But if you think about it, an animal rights person for a dirty little grasshopper! I mean, that's a bit ridiculous, don't you think? I think they should be helping some homeless people or something . . .'

What's Eating Gilbert Grape? producer Alan C. Blomquist was amazed by what Leonardo – in only his second big film role – was able to do with such a difficult and challenging character: 'Leonardo gives Arnie this childlike quality, playing him very free and open and honest. He's a great counterpart to Johnny's Gilbert, who is so solemn and serious about life.'

For Leonardo, Depp was a potential role model, an actor just over ten years his senior who knew a thing or two about the Hollywood system and the capricious

'We had a brotherly
relationship,' said
Leonardo of his
work with Johnny
Depp in What's
Eating Gilbert
Grape?

nature of fame. At nineteen and on only his second mainstream film, Leonardo was on a steep learning curve as far as film acting went and he was grateful for any guidance or tips he could get from his co-stars. As he had done with DeNiro, Leonardo set out to learn as much as he could from Depp, absorbing knowledge, tricks and skills from his co-stars on each of his movies, allowing him to broaden his range and so deepen his portrayals of characters.

'We had a brotherly relationship on camera,' recalled Leonardo of working with Depp in Austin, Texas, where the movie was shot, 'so it was important to just be buddy-buddy with each other. Brothers don't necessarily have to say anything to each other – they can sit in a room and be together and just be completely comfortable with each

'Brothers don't necessarily have to say anything to each other – they can sit in a room and be together and just be completely comfortable with each other.'

other.'

Depp was also very interested in Leonardo – and particularly in his repertoire of bizarre faces. As filming progressed and the diversions offered in remote Austin rapidly began to pale, Depp took to grossing Leonardo out, simply to see him pull a funny face. 'Johnny loved to see my facial expressions when I was disgusted by something gross,' recalled Leonardo of the pair's attempts at amusing themselves off camera. Although it may have been fun during the long waits between set-ups, these pranks showed Leonardo's continuing inability to control his childlike tendencies off-screen, as well as his restless nature and inability to concentrate on the job at hand. 'He'd give me stuff to smell – like decaying honeycomb, rotten eggs and pickled sausage – and I would do

*Juliette Lewis called
Leonardo 'my
little pal'.*

this gagging thing. In the end I couldn't stand it and charged him for the pleasure. I made about $500. The egg embryos were the big bomber – I got a hundred or two hundred bucks for that. I was disgusted. Johnny just loves to laugh, I guess.'

The last laugh was on Depp, as after the film was released it was Leonardo and not Depp who won the acclaim and was nominated for a Best Supporting Actor Oscar, as well as winning the New Generation Award again and the National Board of Review Award.

However, Leonardo was not to win that 1994 Oscar, however much it was deserved. Instead the award went to Tommy Lee Jones for his role in *The Fugitive*, a move by the Academy widely recognised as a way of rewarding time served, rather than actually weighing up the relative performances on their merits. Leonardo was not even expecting a nomination, so the young actor was not too disappointed at not winning first time out. For him, the nomination was enough at this stage in his career. 'I was asleep when it was announced. My agent called me and said: "You've got it! You've got it!" And I said: "Great. Great." And then I went right back to bed. Actually, if you must know I've become really conceited – just kidding. Since then, I've

'I was dreading winning. I didn't even plan a speech – I was worried that I would slip up or do something horrible. I was shaking in my seat, putting on a posed smile. Inside I was petrified.'

been getting a lot more phone calls. My answering machine has a bigger tape in it.'

Despite not expecting to win, the ceremony itself was a gruelling experience for Leonardo, who attended with his mother, father and stepmother – a female bodybuilder. 'I was dreading winning. I didn't even plan a speech – I was worried that I would slip up or do something horrible. I was shaking in my seat, putting on a posed smile. Inside I was petrified.' Despite his mother almost missing Leonardo's big moment, the evening went off without a hitch for the family.

The Oscar nomination and the pair of performances in *This Boy's Life* and *What's Eating Gilbert Grape?* meant Leonardo DiCaprio had arrived on the Hollywood map at the tender age of nineteen. Casting agents began to sit up and take notice of the newest young actor in their midst, and Leonardo found himself touted for many parts, whether he was suitable or not.

The sudden burst of interest led to a great deal of caution on the actor's part. He waited over a year before agreeing to take on a new role after *What's Eating Gilbert Grape?* This was partly due to his being more selective in the roles he accepted, but there was also an element of fear as the young actor wondered whether his two acclaimed performances could be repeated or if he was a one-off, flash-in-the-pan actor.

'I didn't know what types of movies I wanted to do. I want to do things that are different. I want to take my time with each role,' he admitted. 'That's how you plan a long career rather than doing it all in one big explosion. I turned down a lot of movies about death and a few cheesy little comedies, but then *The Quick And The Dead* and *The Basketball Diaries* came along.' He knew enough at such a young age not to jump at the first role offered, but he also knew it was wise to strike while the iron was hot and he was in demand.

This cautious strategy served Leonardo well, and he avoided some high profile

roles which may have done him more damage in the long term – like that of superhero sidekick Robin in *Batman Forever*, a part taken by Chris O'Donnell. 'I couldn't deal with playing a character who rides motorcycles and has a leather jacket and is a tough kid, y'know? There's the stamp of stereotypical right there. It's, like, can you think of anything more obvious? It's hard to explain, but I'm just sick of the heroic man-figure that thinks they're perfect. I want to do some pretty crazy stuff. I just like the idea of doing more of the unplanned stuff.'

Leonardo's approach to his career – like much of the acting skill he displays in his movies – would be expected of someone twice his age, not someone who, in 1994, was on the verge of his twentieth birthday. 'I just don't want to be big box office just yet,' he said, determined to avoid the easy Hollywood route to fame and fortune. 'The more you stay low key at a young age, the more you have room for that stuff in the future, and as long as I can maintain doing films that I want to do, then I'd rather not

Leonardo at the premiere of What's Eating Gilbert Grape? *with co-stars, Juliette Lewis and Laura Harrington.*

'I didn't know what types of movies I wanted to do. I want to do things that are different. I want to take my time with each role.'

blow my load on the work. It seems like a lot of people who try to do that disappear.'

From his initial financial motivation to become an actor after envying his step-brother's pay packet of $50,000 for an advert, Leonardo had progressed to working out a rough game plan for his career. 'Before I started, I had this view that I was going to do one film a year, and that it was going to be a fantastic film. I still think I want to limit myself to not working all the time, 'cause that's not good for my career, but mainly I'm just trying to be selective and to cut through the bullshit hype about scripts, and what everyone else is telling me to do. It's a really hard thing to learn, and I haven't mastered it yet, but I just want to keep on doing stuff that hasn't been done before.'

Newly famous after *What's Eating Gilbert Grape?*, Leonardo had to adjust to a whole new way of life. His initial approach was to try not to change, but he still had to adjust his lifestyle nevertheless. 'I don't want to become a strange person. I don't want to give up the life I already have. My career should adapt to me. Fame is like a VIP pass wherever you want to go,' said Hollywood's newest film star.

Nothing changed immediately. Leonardo stayed living with his mum in Los Feliz. He didn't splash out, saving and investing his new found cash, allowing his parents to handle his business affairs, saying: 'I've managed to keep a clear head and remain sane in this business because I remain a kid off-camera.' His father, George, was taken aback by his son's sudden success: 'We think he's actually an alien. There's something going on in him that we don't understand.'

Leonardo was keen to play the western hero in The Quick And The Dead.

'I've managed to keep a clear head and remain sane in this business because I remain a kid off-camera.'

Leonardo's rise from TV shows to major movies had given him a public persona and he found it altered how he was in private. 'I've changed,' he admitted. 'You can't help it. Your mind starts working in a different way. You feel really scrutinised by people.' Despite having to adjust to a new way of life, Leonardo was determined to hang onto those friends he still knew from his early days in east Hollywood. 'Oh yeah, once I became famous I just dumped all my old friends,' Leonardo joked to *Premiere* magazine. 'I just laid down the law: "Hey, I'm sorry, you can't be part of my new cool life." You just gotta be firm with those people.' His continuing connections with old friends even resulted in him creating employment for one. 'I get a friend to travel with me. I'm paying my friend Jonah to be my assistant. I need somebody to bring me back to who I am. It's hard to be alone.'

Soon the press had started looking for stories about Leonardo, talking to his friends, his neighbours and people who he hadn't seen in years. The stories were not always pleasant or even true as journalists looked for any hint of scandal in the DiCaprio household. One incident saw a writer from a national American newspaper come to the house in Los Feliz which Leonardo still shared with his mother, Irmelin. Welcoming the journalist, the family treated him as a guest, providing a guided tour, including Leonardo's room, and the stash of fan mail stored in the garage. 'Then we read the article,' said Leonardo, still angry about the incident, 'and it says, "Irmelin DiCaprio takes me into the back, takes out a big fat joint, lights it up, takes two big hits and blows out as she walks back into the living room." And you know, it's not the principle of the pot, it's just the principle of the lie. Marijuana's not that big a deal, you know, I don't give a shit, but the fact that someone I was nice to takes it into their head to invent something out of nothing, and said those things about my mother really pissed me off. She was so upset about it.' It was a tough way to learn about the sometimes unscrupulous nature of the press but Leonardo would be more prepared in future dealings with interviewers.

'I couldn't deal with playing a character who rides motorcycles and has a leather jacket and is a tough kid, y'know?'

He also had to deal with a phenomenon new to him – fans. 'I guess this fame thing is hard. Not that I mind being recognised, but suddenly all these teenage girls have become hysterical, man. What they do is shocking, climbing over walls and stuff. I'm recognised more than I was before, and I'm adapting to that. I went to the mall the other day and I noticed a lot more eyes trailing me. I thought, "Do they recognise me, or do they just think I'm weird?" That's

hard to adjust to.'

Money was another big benefit of Leonardo's stardom – after all, it was his original desire to emulate his stepbrother Adam's advertising earnings that made him investigate acting in the first place. 'If you're going to talk about money, I'm the cheapest bastard in the world. I mean, I never let people borrow money or anything. I'm still making savings and stuff. I plan on investing it, just keeping it for when I'm older. You never know, I may go bankrupt, or lose my career, or have a Hugh Grant situation. Then I'll have some dough.'

His success in two acclaimed films had been astonishing, but Leonardo was still not confident that even he understood how he put his craft into motion or where his talents came from. However he did it, he was still not convinced that DeNiro's method acting route – which he'd employed to great effect on *What's Eating Gilbert Grape?* – was for him. 'I would have a nervous breakdown if I had to go through a movie for three months and be that character on and off set. I know what I'm doing, but when they say "Cut", I'm fine. I can

'I've changed. You can't help it. Your mind starts working in a different way. You feel really scrutinised by people.'

joke around. I don't go hide in the corner and yell at anyone who tries to speak to me . . .'

After turning down a role in the Bette Midler film *Hocus Pocus*, Leonardo made a pitch to replace the late River Phoenix in the role of the Interviewer in Neil Jordan's film version of Anne Rice's novel *Interview With The Vampire*. He auditioned for the role, impressing the director and producer David Geffen, but they ultimately decided that Leonardo was just too young and gave the part to Christian Slater instead. It wasn't to be the last time that Leonardo would be considered for a role originally offered to River Phoenix.

Not doing *Interview With The Vampire* allowed Leonardo to make one of the odder items on his filmography – a 27-minute short titled *The Foot Shooting Party*, made in 1994. Leonardo plays a young rock'n'roll singer who tries to escape the draft for the Vietnam War in the early seventies by shooting himself in the foot. However, he finds pulling the trigger is harder than he had thought it might be. Bellbottoms and hair extensions allowed Leonardo to get into character for an era that was coming to an end when he was born.

The film was financed by Touchstone – part of the Disney empire – from their discretionary incentive fund. The fund aimed to finance short films made by potential feature film directors who'd had no previous directorial experience. The short training film was directed by newcomer Annette Haywood-Carter. Leonardo accepted the part as an acting exercise which allowed him to metaphorically stretch his dramatic muscles. Not sure of his abilities or how he achieved the considerable effects he did on screen, Leonardo was open to testing his talents in the short film format before embarking on another full-length feature film.

'The movies I'm doing are basically my drama school,' he admitted, candidly. 'Working with people like Robert DeNiro. I watched him intensely all the time. All I know is the things I say to myself first-hand when I'm doing it and that is to be present in the character and constantly kick myself in the ass in focusing on what this character's really feeling.' Leonardo recognised he was still a student, learning the art and craft of film acting to supplement the natural talent he had in spades.

Returning to feature films, Leonardo DiCaprio found himself moving temporarily from Los Angeles to Mescal in Arizona to play the part of The Kid in Sam Raimi's violent reworking of the classic western genre, *The Quick And The Dead*. Shooting took place on the western town set which had been built for the 1968 Lee Marvin film *Monte Walsh* and used in over 50 other westerns. *The Quick And The Dead* revolves around the staging of a to-the-death gunfighting contest held in the back-of-beyond desert town of Redemption. The town is lorded over by Herod (Gene Hackman), who runs the deadly gunfights and collects 50 per cent tax from all the residents. He's not exactly Mr Popular. As the competition approaches, a *Who's Who* of western villainy ride into town, all aiming to be the one who survives to claim the prize. Two strangers stand out among the crowd – one for his youth and the other for her sex. The Kid (Leonardo) claims to be Herod's son, determined to face him in a gunfight on Redemption's Main Street. Ellen's (Sharon Stone) reasons for wanting to take up the gun remain a mystery until the dramatic climax of the film.

For Leonardo, the film was not straight-forwardly attractive. 'I rejected it many times because I thought it was just going to be a commercial film. Sharon Stone and everything. But then, with one day to decide, I said "OK". I like Sam Raimi and this character's really funny and cool.' Additionally, the actor who was still a big kid at heart couldn't resist the temptation to dress up as a cowboy and run around on a genuine western street set, playing at gunfights.

Stone – in her role as co-producer – was determined to have Leonardo in the film. 'I wanted him bad, and we'd topped out financially,' said Stone, explaining how she personally came up with some of the money to pay for Leonardo. She had to stand back and hope for the best from her investment. 'It better [work out], or I'm going to beat the living shit out of him,' she confided to *Premiere* magazine. '"You little punk, I want my money back".'

Her power-broking did not please everyone involved in the production, but when she put her money where her mouth was, attitudes changed. 'I helped fund that film and they tried to shut me out,' said Stone of the studio suits. 'I think that when you come in as an actress, they're certain you're just there to torture them. Then, when I paid for half of Leonardo DiCaprio's salary, they got over it.'

Unusual as this financial arrangement was, Stone believed that her money was spent in the best interests of the film. 'He was worth it,' she said of Leonardo. 'He's smart and talented beyond belief.'

For director Sam Raimi, Leonardo was the ideal actor to capture the innocence of the Kid. 'He's the embodiment of wild youth,' said Raimi of his young star. 'The Kid thinks he can't die. All he want's out of life is his father's respect. He'll go to any lengths

'I get a friend to travel with me . . . I need somebody to bring me back to who I am. It's hard to be alone.'

for that recognition.'

Having been initially reluctant to take on the role, once on board Leonardo was immersed in his western character. 'I see the Kid as a sort of good version of Billy the Kid. He's cocky and confident, until he gets around his father. Then he just begs for attention by trying to prove he can kill faster and better than anyone else in town. He's a sad case, but a really interesting character to play.' It was to be Leonardo's first movie death scene, but not his last.

The expected romantic entanglement between Sharon Stone and Leonardo

DiCaprio was a brief scene that neither party seems to have enjoyed much. 'Everyone's making such a big deal out of it,' lamented Leonardo at the time. 'It really wasn't much of anything. She shoots this guy, then grabs me by the back of the neck and kisses me and then flings me off. It wasn't passionate. Very brief and really nothing to talk about.'

Despite what the actor's respective fans might have expected, the pair did not enjoy a dramatic romance during the film. Their one remaining kiss – another was cut from the final film – didn't seem to impress Leonardo much, either. 'I was expecting a little more from ol' Sharon, y'know? I wasn't about to get down and dirty with her, so it was a bit of a let down. Actually, she hurt my lip.'

During promotional work for the film, when asked what he thought of Sharon Stone, Leonardo famously commented that she was 'better than a bag of snot'. It was his puerile attempt to escape the usual film promotion glibness when talking about co-stars, but it showed he still hadn't learned the most advantageous way of dealing with the press. It was also another sign of the childish immaturity which was such an asset to his acting on screen, but such a liability when he tried to be clever or funny off screen. He would repeat such childish quips on future film promotion tours. 'I couldn't just say I like her and say she was cool. I had to contradict the bad press she'd gotten. I could never just say "I respect her" because that would

'I rejected it many times because I thought it was just going to be a commercial film. Sharon Stone and everything. But then, with one day to decide, I said "OK". I like Sam Raimi and this character's really funny and cool.'

be boring. Gotta add a little spice to it, a little flipside, a little whatever . . .'

Despite their best efforts to promote the movie, and the fact that Stone had put up her own cash for part of the budget, *The Quick And The Dead* was not a big hit. On a budget of $32 million, the first run US gross barely reached $20 million, although the film became something of a cult item on video, in keeping with other Sam Raimi movies.

Sharon Stone's career may have been slightly set back by the film's failure, but it didn't seem to affect Leonardo, who was philosophical about it all. 'I don't regret it,' he said of his performance in *The Quick And The Dead*. 'It's not my favourite film in the world. I guess it was not that good. It was alright, you know. I had a good time doing the character.'

Rumours of an affair on set between Leonardo and his co-star Sharon Stone which hit the press during the production of the film were unfounded, according to the actor. 'Look, I worked with Sharon Stone and we're friends – just friends. If I'm seen with any woman, people assume I'm sleeping with them.' It was to be a foretaste

'I was expecting a little more from ol' Sharon, y'know? I wasn't about to get down and dirty with her, so it was a bit of a let down. Actually, she hurt my lip.'

of scandals to come when Leonardo's name was later linked with actress Demi Moore. As a result of his double bill in *What's Eating Gilbert Grape?* and *The Quick And The Dead*, Leonardo DiCaprio had gained even more attention. He was now a genuine film star, in demand by directors, acclaimed by critics and adored by the audience. He resolved not to let his increasing success go to his teenage head. 'Sharon Stone gave me a good piece of advice, "When you're famous you got to accept it as an advantage. It will only make you stronger",' claimed Leonardo. 'I mean, I haven't gone crazy yet, and I really do think I'm pretty well balanced being in the position I'm in. I think it has to do with me not investing everything in my job. All these actors think that the blood through their veins is fuelled by acting. I'm happier when I'm not working, hanging out with my friends, doing something I love.'

Leonardo was still determined to continue to live as normal a life as possible when not making movies. For him fame was just part of the job – and that's all movie making was to be: a job. 'I go places all the time. I'm looking in the *LA Weekly* every week just to find out what stuff there is to do. It still seems like the same life – it really does. I'm not really that widely recognised, which is kinda cool. Maybe I'm a little bit more of a homebody now.'

He was aware, though, that no matter how much he tried to preserve his 'old life', things would never really be the same for him again. 'I want to be a jerk like the rest of my friends, and have fun, and not care about the consequences, but I just can't now.' After all, Leonardo had seen the consequences of infamy at close hand – his doctor was the father of celebrated Hollywood madam Heidi Fleiss, while his dentist was Ewan Chandler, the father of the young boy who accused Michael Jackson of molesting him. Even though he knew there were limits to what he could do, as he was in the public eye, there were many silly things that Leonardo wished he could get away with, in his continuing need to act like a child. 'I'm starting to become appreciative of the things that are happening. I want people my age to believe in something, because I think that's really lacking. I really like to act like a little kid a lot. That's probably one of the truest joys of my life, to act like a little child.'

The interruptions to his life from fans of his work were regarded by Leonardo as being a small price to pay for the financial success and critical acclaim he was enjoying. Talking to fans and signing autographs gave him a concrete connection with his audiences and made him aware of just who he was making the films for. 'A lot of actors have problems with people approaching them, but I've never minded it. What's the worst thing that could happen? Unless someone's going to be violent, the worst is that somebody's going to want an autograph, or shake your hand, or talk to you for a couple of seconds – and that's never harmed anyone. It's a small price to pay for the kind of work I get to do. I know I've had more fun being famous that I would've had otherwise.' Leonardo had fulfilled his need for attention, and the rules of behaviour for someone in the public eye brought him some of the discipline which had been absent during his upbringing.

Aware of the now forgotten flash-in-the-pan young performers who had preceded him, Leonardo was determined to build a lasting career for himself. 'I'm not saying I'm above the rest or I'll only work with big co-stars, but I do have guidelines,' said Leonardo of his process for selecting roles – something he had to develop quickly as he found more and more parts being offered to him. 'There are people who have gotten good roles at my age and their careers later slowed down. Meaning no disrespect to anybody, but I want to avoid that by holding out for only high quality projects. I've set a standard and I hope I don't sell out and end up making stupid stuff.'

From his breakthrough in *What's Eating Gilbert Grape?*, Leonardo had not only secured the part in *The Quick And The Dead*, but also signed up for the role of French poet Rimbaud in the biopic *Total Eclipse*, against the advice of his agents, and a supporting role in the soapy drama *Marvin's Room*. Although he rapidly made the most of his opportunities, Leonardo was determined not to overstretch himself: 'You just get the feeling all the time that you've gotta have more, and no matter how good it is, it's never enough. It's weird – I think the public expects that from you. They want

'I want to be a jerk like the rest of my friends, and have fun, and not care about the consequences, but I just can't now.'

you to keep going, otherwise you could fade away.'

Fading away was not a fate about to befall Leonardo DiCaprio. His trio of critically successful films meant he had a full diary for the next couple of years. His success had brought him plenty of offers including the challenge of playing drug-addict poet Jim Caroll in *The Basketball Diaries*. There was only one cloud on the horizon – his role as French poet Rimbaud in *Total Eclipse* would be dubbed by *Screen International* as a 'potentially career damaging performance'.

This Actor's Life

*'The good thing about acting is that it always keeps you
on your toes . . . It's not like any other job where you
can go in and do the same thing as yesterday.'*

Leonardo DiCaprio

HAVING MADE A DRAMATIC IMPACT ON HOLLYWOOD in only three mainstream performances, Leonardo DiCaprio confounded his admirers by taking part in two projects that a lesser young actor might have considered commercial suicide. Both drugs drama *The Basketball Diaries* and period true story *Total Eclipse* were to bring Leonardo problems, but first he had to deal with the growing rumours about his private life.

Leonardo was linked with young actress Alicia Silverstone, the star of *Clueless* and *The Crush*, and later Batgirl in *Batman & Robin*. Newspapers and magazines claimed the twenty-year-old Leonardo and eighteen-year-old Silverstone were engaged in a secret affair. In fact, the pair had been friends since Silverstone had arrived in Hollywood and begun acting. 'Alicia and I did our first movies at about the same time,' said Leonardo. 'We've known each other for years. I'm sure she was asked this question and she thought it ridiculous.'

Silverstone had found it difficult to cope with her sudden fame and had been attending a quasi-religious course about coping with stress at The Forum in Los Angeles. Leonardo attended the course, too, in order to support Silverstone. 'I just tried it because I wanted to see what it was like,' he claimed. 'They just get you to a point where you realise that everything is nothing, if I can sum it up. And then from there you just create what you want to create. It gave me some different information on how to process stuff. I'm always curious to learn about what there is to learn out there. It's not like Scientology or whatever.' It was there he met and began going out with a young girl named Caitlin. Sometimes the three of them would make an evening of it. It wasn't to be the last time that Leonardo's supposed relationships with other actresses would hit the headlines.

'It's a tough thing – you get in a situation where you feel that you have to be perfect all the time and it sucks.'

The opportunity to star as Jim Carroll in the drugs drama *The Basketball Diaries* came to Leonardo through a drug-related tragedy – the death of young actor River Phoenix,

'Drugs? Everybody has a choice and I choose not to do drugs . . .'

Mickey (Mark Wahlberg) and Jim (Leonardo) discover their friendship cannot survive the descent into drug addition in The Basketball Diaries.

whom Leonardo had lobbied to replace in *Interview With The Vampire.*

Five months before the Oscar ceremony at which Leonardo waited tensely to see if he had won the award for Best Supporting Actor for *What's Eating Gilbert Grape?*, 23-year-old River Phoenix died of a drugs overdose. He collapsed and died in the early hours of 31 October 1993 on the Sunset Boulevard sidewalk outside Johnny Depp's Viper Room club. Phoenix had also been nominated, like Leonardo, for a Best Supporting Actor Oscar, for his role in *Running On Empty*, and like Leonardo he lost to an older, more experienced actor, in his case Kevin Kline. Phoenix seemed the least likely member of the new, young Hollywood 'brat pack' to succumb to the live fast and die young syndrome. From his unusual, itinerant, South American childhood with his hippie parents and unruly siblings, Phoenix had grown up in front of the camera, from his podgy nerd in Joe Dante's *Explorers* to his surprising decision to play a gay hustler alongside heart-throb Keanu Reeves in Gus Van Sant's controversial drama *My Own Private Idaho.* Clearly, some of Phoenix's determination to choose a wide range of unusual roles had rubbed off on Leonardo.

There was more than a passing similarity between the two actors. They both had unconventional parents who took full advantage of the sixties, enjoyed early success in dramatic roles, and later took risks with their careers by playing gay characters. They grew up on screen and gained a huge fan following due to their baby-faced good looks. Despite this, Leonardo was none too happy at being dubbed "the new River Phoenix": 'I think that River was one of the most talented actors in the business and for something like that to happen to him is tragic. It irks me . . . I can't imagine what

Leonardo faced a series of new acting challenges in The Basketball Diaries.

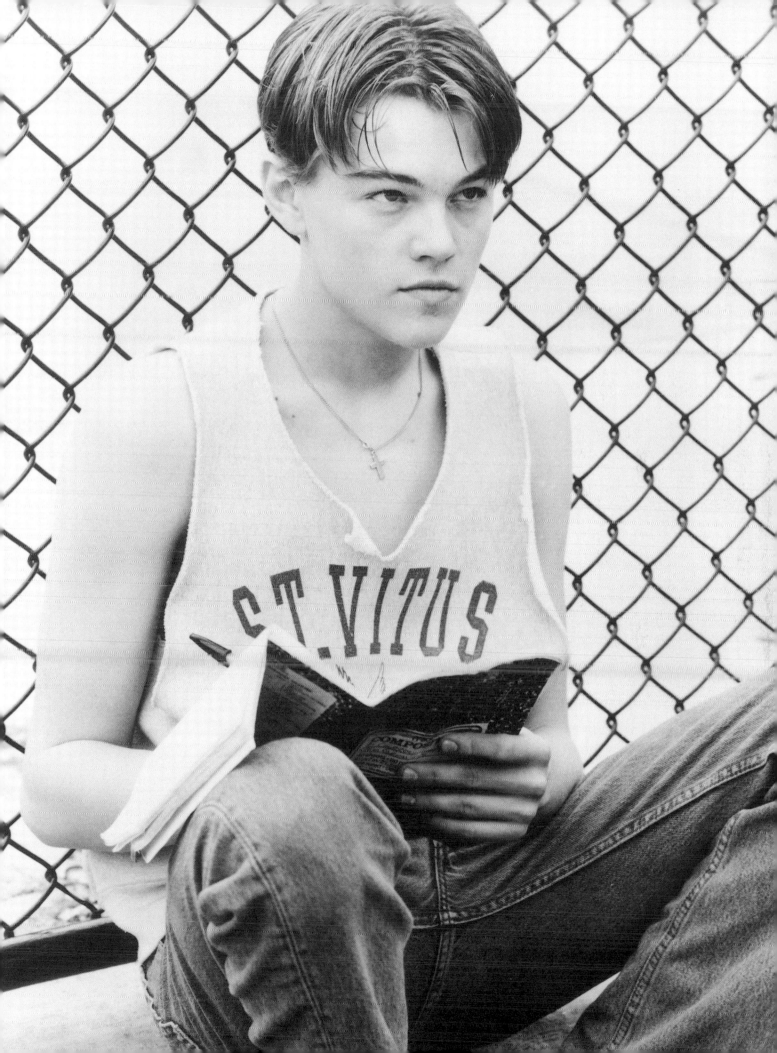

'I touched on emotions I've
never tapped in my entire life.
I've heard a lot of people say,
"I hope this movie doesn't
glamorise drugs" . . .'

possessed him. Too many people think that once you're successful, everything's trippin' dandy, but people get affected by it. I don't know what his problems were, but it's sad we had to lose him like that.'

Leonardo had always wanted to meet Phoenix – and claims to have almost done so on the night of his death. Aged nineteen, Leonardo was celebrating Hallowe'en in style, attending a fancy dress party in Los Angeles. He was dressed as 'Johnny Hollywood' – 'you know, the typical Hollywood actor' – complete with slicked back hair and black leather jacket for posing in. As Leonardo was going into one party venue, he claims to have spotted Phoenix heading in the other direction, leaving for his final, fatal trip to the Viper Room. 'I remember seeing this guy wearing a mask,' said Leonardo. 'I knew it was River. I wanted to say "Hi", but I got caught up in a crowd and slid right past him. Next thing I knew, River had died; that same night.'

The Basketball Diaries has it's origins in the true life story of sixties poet Jim Carroll. His autobiographical account of a teenager's descent into the horrors of drug addiction caught reader's imaginations when first published in *The Paris Review* in the late sixties. It wasn't until 1978 that the story appeared in book form, which lead to immediate interest from film-makers. It wasn't to be until much later, in 1994, that a film of the harrowing tale finally made it into production.

'When a role for a young guy is being offered to me, I think of River Phoenix. It feels like a loss.'

Over the years many young up-and-coming stars had been attached to the project, including Matt Dillon (who gave his best performance in Gus Van Sant's *Drugstore Cowboy*), Eric Stoltz, Anthony Michael Hall and finally River Phoenix. The Reagan/Bush war on drugs and frequent changes of decision-making personnel in Hollywood served to delay the production of the sure-to-be controversial film. Phoenix's drug-related death didn't help its prospects much, either.

It was the interest of director Scott Kalvert, whose background had been in pop videos and the title sequence for Will Smith's hit TV series *The Fresh Prince Of Bel Air*, that served to kick start the project once again. Although the original material had been written 30 years before, Kalvert recognised that the story *The Basketball Diaries* had to tell was as relevant in the nineties as it had been in the sixties. He knew the latest version of the script had to be a contemporary story drawing on the same source material, so he updated the settings, but kept the core characters.

The next task for Kalvert and screenwriter Bryan Golubuff was to fill the central role of Jim Carroll now that their first choice was no longer available. Enough time had passed since the inception of the film for Leonardo DiCaprio to be about the right age for the role. He in turn was fascinated by the affecting material. 'It's rare when you find something this raw,' recalled Leonardo of reading the screenplay. 'Writing so completely honest that after reading it, you know the person – the way they are, the way they thought, what they went through.'

The Basketball Diaries depicts the downfall of a group of school friends, all part of the church basketball team, who are drawn into a life of crime and hustling when they get involved in drugs. Alongside Leonardo as Jim Carroll were Mark Whalberg (better known as Calvin Klein model and rap star Marky Mark), James Madio and Patrick McGaw as Carroll's friends in addiction. Actress Lorraine Bracco, best known for her role in *Goodfellas*, played Carroll's long suffering mother, while *Ghostbusters'* Ernie Hudson was Carroll's father figure who sees the young man through his detox period – the most harrowing section in the movie which shows Leonardo to be a confident young actor at the peak of his powers.

Drugs had not been part of Leonardo's own experience – and in the light of what had befallen River Phoenix, he was ever more determined to keep it that way. 'Drugs? Everybody has a choice and I choose not to do drugs. Period. I don't do drugs and I never have. I hate them and I've seen the effects of what they do since I was very young,' he said, recalling his early days in the seedy side of east Hollywood. 'The only drugs I've tried are marijuana and alcohol and I haven't [done] marijuana for a year, 'cause it makes me sad, it makes me think about all the bad things in my life. A big reason why I did *The Basketball Diaries* was the fact that there's such a ridiculous heroin craze going on right now, and it's so sad.' Leonardo saw his role in the film as a chance to get a message across to young people his own age, who could be watching and might be in a similar position to his character – tempted by the drugs scene: 'I was making a statement against drugs.'

Another attraction for Leonardo in taking on the role was the opportunity to live out and live through some of Jim Carroll's experiences without having to take the same risks. It was one of the perks of movie making. 'The fact that we were allowed to do all these bad things in this film, that appealed to me. That's why the film is so great – because you can play a character and not suffer the consequences of your actions. But of course, not everything in the film is something I want to do personally. I don't want to get addicted to heroin.'

Whatever his personal views on drug use, Leonardo faced one of the toughest acting challenges in his career to date – how to convincingly play someone on drugs. 'I looked at it as an acting challenge. I knew the basics – what makes you hyper, what makes you drowsy. I relied on a counsellor to learn about the specific behavioural nuances. After all, I don't have to be retarded to play a retarded person.'

Despite his in-depth research on *What's Eating Gilbert Grape?*, Leonardo claimed not to be into method acting, but he did indulge in a degree of research for his role as Jim Carroll. He was, after all, playing a real life person. The counsellor was an ex-drug addict assigned by the studio to Leonardo to help him develop his performance, particularly for the central cold turkey scenes. He also spent a good deal of time with Jim Carroll, discussing his experiences and talking through each stage of how he coped with his addiction. 'When Jim withdraws from drugs, he becomes an animal,' said Leonardo of the scenes which displayed the full range of the young actor's extraordinary acting talents. 'I touched on emotions I've never tapped in my entire life. I've heard a lot of people say, "I hope this movie doesn't glamorise drugs." I think it will show how easy it is to get addicted, and how once you give yourself a reason to take that first hit you can get in over your head. This film shows the destruction and consequences of taking that first hit.'

'I've always been spontaneous and outgoing . . . I've tried lots of things so I've got some good life experiences, which is great 'cause it means I've got lots of material to work with as an actor.'

Although Leonardo was not too daunted by the acting challenges of playing the drug scenes, delivering some of Carroll's poetry before a live audience proved to be another matter. The sequence which sees Carroll successfully turn his experiences into a performance reading proved to be the most difficult for Leonardo to tackle. 'I can't focus on doing really long speeches,' admitted the actor who feels the need to be perfect in every role he tackles. 'Looking out to an audience and trying to act at the same time – I got sort of dyslexic. And Lorraine Bracco was like "It's all right, calm down, it's not that big a deal, do it tomorrow if you can't do it today." And it's a tough thing – you get in

a situation where you feel that you have to be perfect all the time and it sucks, it really does. Sometimes you just sit there and go: "Jesus, I don't know what to do".'

Leonardo's acting was so convincing it had some newspaper writers thinking he really was doing drugs during the movie, despite claims that all anyone ever snorted on set was chocolate ovaltine. 'People confused me with my part and told stories about me having a drug habit. It just makes me mad to have other people think I have something to hide,' responded Leonardo to the accusations. While realising he was less than perfect, Leonardo had no wish for people to believe he was another River Phoenix. 'I really don't have that much to hide. Not as far as the typical things, the stereotype that's coming with a young Hollywood actor. Give or take the cockiness, the joking around, the wanting to go and have fun, meet people, whatever. All that's there, but as far as all that other crap that comes with it, it really doesn't apply to me and it makes me angry. I hate it when it's insinuated . . . if I read "whispers of heroin use", things like that eat at me.'

While he was shooting *The Basketball Diaries* in New York City, Leonardo found himself becoming a regular in the gossip columns, supposedly clubbing and brawling his way through the New York nights. According to reports, the young actor was spotted with everyone from *What's Eating Gilbert Grape?* star Juliette Lewis to

'The role of Rimbaud is one of the most important of my career and one of the best roles to play for a young actor.'

Ralph Lauren teen supermodel Bridget Hall. Gossip Liz Smith wrote: 'He seldom sleeps, so intense is his partying.' He was also named as a regular partner with the model Bijou Phillips, half-sister to 'model-actress-whatever' Chynna Phillips.

Leonardo insists that the tabloids greatly exaggerated his trips out and about, which amounted to the kind of ordinary evenings everyone enjoys as part of New York's night life. 'Bridget Hall and I hung out for a week. The whole thing was blown out of proportion. I'm written up in the tabloids because I go out to places. I won't stay cooped up in my hotel room. Most famous people aren't out and about. I just think I'm a 22-year-old guy who wants to live out his youth and do films at the same time. Having fun is a huge priority for me, whatever gets said about it. I know where the line is, and when not to go over it.'

Whatever he got up to off-screen, his on-screen portrayal of a young man in the grip of a demon addiction was convincing enough for the critics, who raved about the film. The *Washington Post* said of *The Basketball Diaries*: 'Hard-eyed and gaunt, Leonardo DiCaprio works hard, as always, at embodying fallen angel Carroll, and he creates one undeniably impressive achievement.' In addition to the critical acclaim, the low budget film, on its first run in the United States, grossed in the region of $2.5

Leonardo was fiercely proud of his work on Total Eclipse.

million, a modest achievement, but a solid showing for a cheap-to-make movie dealing with such a controversial subject.

Growing up on screen had meant that Leonardo's teenage years were far from ordinary. He had more money than most, for a start. Not many who are on the verge of turning twenty can buy a silver BMW coupe on a whim, as Leonardo did. The attentions of his fans also marked Leonardo out for special treatment. Although he tried to maintain an ordinary life, it became more difficult as he became better known. It was his continual need to play, to mimic and imitate, which had allowed Leonardo to give such depth to his early performances. That had come from his background – his unprivileged childhood and indulgent, laid-back parents. It had all helped in his acting, but he was still working at developing his real-life self away from the movie cameras.

'It was the simple fact that there was probably not a cooler character on earth that I could play . . .'

Now he was rich and famous, Leonardo remembered his humble beginnings and set out to help children who were living in poverty as he had done. Charity became a big part of Leonardo's focus, as he donated food and clothes to homeless charities, attended fund-raising benefits for AIDS charities and always gave generously. Closest to his heart was his work for children and animals. He visited sick children who were staying in Ronald McDonald House, a facility sponsored by the burger giant, and he gave funds to a campaign to save the Manatees in Florida, whose numbers were being severely reduced due to boating and fishing in the area. He had always been interested in sea life and conservation of dying species, and now he had the opportunity to do something about it. These activities were his way of giving something back in return for the fame and good fortune he'd received. He preferred to do this work in private rather than become publicly identified with a cause as to him it felt 'realer' the fewer people who knew about it.

'I've always been spontaneous and outgoing,' said Leonardo of his nature, attributes which helped his natural acting ability. 'I've tried lots of things so I've got some good life experiences, which is great 'cause it means I've got lots of material to work with as an actor.' Now firmly part of the Hollywood movie star mainstream, Leonardo was in danger of losing touch with those 'life experiences' which fed his performances. His life had changed and so had his experiences, events which were bound to lead to changes in the Leonardo DiCaprio who appeared on movie screens.

'There is homosexuality, but the film's not about that . . . It's about a young guy who wanted to experience everything and that was just one element of many that was there for him to partake in.'

At the end of September 1995 Leonardo received what must have been the first bad notice of his relatively blessed career. A review in *Screen International* of *Total Eclipse* noted: 'As portrayed by Leonardo DiCaprio, in a potentially career-damaging performance, Rimbaud is a feral savant, suicidally uninhibited, endlessly annoying.'

It was a review that was given short shrift by the actor himself: 'I can't listen to that kind of shit. So the article said "career-damaging", huh? I really don't think it's gonna be career damaging, and if it is, then fuck everybody. I'm proud of my work in all the movies I've done. In a few years' time no one will remember the bad reviews; those films will be seen as part of the body of my work.'

For Leonardo the choice of such a provocative role was deliberate. 'The role of Rimbaud is one of the most important of my career and one of the best roles to play for a young actor. Rimbaud wanted to change the world from one day to the next. He was someone courageous, who didn't worry about the consequences of his actions. I live my life thinking of the consequences. Shooting this film, I learned not to worry about what others thought of what I was doing. It wasn't easy, but it changed me.'

The attraction of the off-beat role for Leonardo was clear in his mind, no matter what the critics or his career advisors might think. 'It was the simple fact that there was probably not a cooler character on earth that I could play. He was just fearless. He was trying to reach the peak of something. He spoke his mind, always, did all kinds of crazy shit. The character turned me on, and it would have been ridiculous for me to turn it down. That's really the question to ask: why wouldn't I do it?'

Set in the 1870s, this audacious, demanding, provocative and fictionalised biographical film tells the tale of the homosexual relationship between French poets Arthur Rimbaud and Paul Verlaine. Born in 1854 in France, as a teenager Rimbaud wrote dark, visionary, romantic poetry which resulted in much acclaim and led to a tempestuous relationship with married fellow writer Verlaine. Later, the pair quarrelled and Rimbaud was shot by Verlaine. After the age of twenty, Rimbaud stopped writing, claiming to be unable to match his earlier achievements. Later years were spent involved in all sorts of bizarre events in Africa, including arms dealing and selling

shoes, before he died at the age of 37 as his leg was amputated. It was not the kind of material to have your run-of-the mill Hollywood heart-throb calling their agent to demand an audition.

For screenwriter Christopher Hampton, the story of Rimbaud had been an obsession since his twenties, one which led to him studying the subject at Oxford, as well as writing and rewriting the original play from 1967 on which the film *Total Eclipse* was based.

Hampton – who also scripted the John Malkovich and Keanu Reeves costume melodrama *Dangerous Liaisons* from one of his own plays – had tried to get a film version made since the early 1970s. 'There were serious conversations on my first trip to Los Angeles in 1970, and there was an excellent BBC TV version in the early seventies, but it wasn't until the end of the eighties that I was approached to write a film to mark the centenary of Rimbaud's death, in 1991.'

Hampton was closely involved in the film in all its incarnations. 'Volker Schlondorff was to direct and John Malkovich seemed ideal for Verlaine. I suggested – having just marvelled at his performance in *My Own Private Idaho* – that River Phoenix should be invited to play Rimbaud. He read the script and agreed: but before we could meet came the tragic news of his death. John [Malkovich] was unable to envisage working with another actor in the role and the whole thing came unravelled.'

According to Hampton, though, these events were all to the good of the final film, opening the way for the casting of Leonardo DiCaprio. 'Agnieszka Holland took it on and reanimated the whole process by casting the marvellous boy, Leonardo DiCaprio, whose uncanny physical resemblance to Rimbaud was the cornerstone of a remarkable performance. Apart from anything else, and unlike many actors who have played the

THE LEONARDO DICAPRIO ALBUM

role, he actually looked no more than sixteen.' Hampton turned his involvement with the film into two on-screen cameo appearances – first as a photographer whom Rimbaud attacks with a swordstick and later as the Belgian judge who sentences Verlaine to imprisonment for immorality.

More than being just another tale of a self-destructive writer, as in *The Basketball Diaries*, the part Leonardo accepted in *Total Eclipse* had another connection with his previous film – he was again taking over a role originally offered to the late River Phoenix. Polish director Agnieszka Holland felt Leonardo was the obvious choice – and his casting changed the movie again. 'When Leonardo accepted, John Malkovich ran out for reasons that are complicated,' admitted Holland. 'The first idea that came into my head was David Thewlis. I had seen him in *Naked* and I needed someone very different [from Leonardo].'

For Leonardo, things couldn't have worked out better. 'When Agnieszka said "We have this guy, David Thewlis," I was like, "Oh My God!",' enthused Leonardo of his new co-star. 'Me and all my friends are huge fans of that movie [*Naked*].' From his ground-breaking performance in the award-winning Mike Leigh London low-life drama, Thewlis had moved to Hollywood and become an English character actor for hire in films such as *Dragonheart* and *Restoration*. *Total Eclipse* was much more in line with the challenging role in the Mike Leigh film that had established his notoriety.

For Leonardo, the film was a whole different matter. 'I learned a lot,' he admitted of the experience, but it wasn't one he was to thoroughly enjoy, finding some of the scenes that were required difficult to perform. 'The movie dealt a lot with the writing and didn't have so much of the drug aspect that *The Basketball Diaries* had. That was really about the physicality of being on drugs and *Total Eclipse* was about the artist's turmoil of wanting to surpass anything he's ever done before, and just not being able to do that because he's a human being. That was totally different to deal with. I don't know as far as depression and thought are concerned, but it definitely had a lot of weird parallels [with *The Basketball Diaries*] – a young writer, the drug thing and a bunch of other things.' It was at this time, inspired by this role and that of Jim Carroll, that Leonardo himself began writing poetry. It is a habit he is secretive about, and he's not willing to share his work with anyone. Whether he is simply playing at the poetry game, or may one day publish a volume of verse, time will tell. The mysterious nature of his poetry, though, did much to boost his image as the sensitive, romantic movie star which he liked to project to the public.

If anything was to give Leonardo pause for thought before committing to *Total Eclipse*, it was the necessary sex scenes between the two lead characters, and it was these scenes which led his agent to advise against doing the film. Since his childhood encounter with 'some major homosexual activity' at the age of five in his poor east Hollywood neighbourhood, Leonardo had admitted it had left 'an imprint on my mind'. Following early rumours about his own sexuality after the kiss in *This Boy's Life*, Leonardo had been wary of playing homosexual characters. It might be too much to suggest that the young actor was homophobic, given the roles he has tackled. After the *This Boy's Life* homosexual kiss there were the gay rent boy scenes in *The Basketball Diaries*, so he was no stranger to that type of material. However, the proposed scenes in *Total Eclipse* were much more up front and physical than either of those two previous films. Since the initial shock and later acclaim dished out to River Phoenix and Keanu Reeves for tackling gay roles in *My Own Private Idaho*, the stigma of playing such parts had been reduced, but Leonardo was, whatever bravado he might project, still worried about the perception of him after the film was finished.

Despite his fears, he felt the need to meet the acting challenges the role presented.

'There is homosexuality, but the film's not about that,' he was quick to claim when the topic was raised. 'It's about a young guy who wanted to experience everything and that was just one element of many that was there for him to partake in.' More perhaps than the aftermath, the actual shooting of these scenes was more troubling to Leonardo than it was for the older, more experienced (and heterosexual) David Thewlis. 'David is just matter-of-fact', said director Agnieszka Holland. 'He helped Leonardo a lot to do the things that were much more difficult for Leonardo. When you are twenty years old, to do that stuff is very risky.'

David Thewlis was much more down to earth about the whole thing, and wondered what Leonardo was making such a big fuss about. 'Certainly if anyone was worried about doing it,' he said, 'then that would call their sexuality into question more than if they did it. It's, like, what are you scared of? That you might like it? So, what if you do?'

'I'm proud of my work in all the movies I've done. In a few years' time no one will remember the bad reviews.'

'There was a sequence of me being sodomised by Leonardo,' confirmed Thewlis. 'When we filmed it, it was hysterical. I'm lying face down on the bed naked, Leo's behind me with a cushion between us, and I'm screaming my head off. I don't know, it was fun! Leo was a little uptight about the homosexuality in the film. He coped with that by being Beavis and Butthead about it.'

Leonardo had strong reservations about the shooting of these scenes and he spoke to Thewlis about them. 'I told him I wasn't thrilled to do it,' he said. 'I wasn't exactly nervous about it, but I was a little queasy. But it was cool . . . David was right there for me. It's difficult because you have to act like you really like it and be convincing. I made sure our lips were clean and everything – I got a little disinfectant. We were a little too close for my taste at times. It wasn't fun, though. David was more relaxed about it than I was. He is the consummate professional and constantly drives himself to do new and different things.'

The experience was not one Leonardo would forget quickly, nor does it seem likely to be one he would want to repeat in the near future. 'Actually, I got very nauseous, as it was my first time kissing a guy. It was like slow motion, know what I mean? I saw his lips coming towards mine and I was like, "Oh Jesus, is this really going to happen?" Nasty. My stomach was seriously turning after this.' Leonardo certainly didn't make this amount of fuss over his kiss with Sharon Stone in *The Quick And The Dead*. '[Thewlis] kept on saying that if you're scared of it, you're homophobic. Well, call me homophobic if you like, but I'm just grossed out by it,' was Leonardo's final comment on the subject.

What was worse for Leonardo was that his mum, Irmelin, was featured as an extra in the movie. She was one of the nurses watching as the 37-year-old Rimbaud (Leonardo in ageing make-up) has his leg amputated after developing a tumour on his knee. The scenes had parallels in Leonardo's off-screen real life at the time as his mother was nursing his ailing grandfather. Blood clots had been forming in Leonardo's grandfather's feet, and amputation of his leg was set for the same day as his grandson's cinematic amputation. In the event, the surgery was postponed due to growths on the old man's stomach. It was to no avail, and his grandfather died in late 1995, soon followed by Leonardo's beloved, but constantly ill, dog Rocky.

'All of this stuff has been going on in my mind,' said Leonardo of shooting the scene. 'My mother's playing a nurse and that's what she's been to my grandfather in the past couple of weeks. My grandfather's always been this really hard man. A German man, a hard worker. And now he's telling everyone that he has a soft heart. And he's saying this on his deathbed . . . I love my grandpa, but that's not what I want to do. I don't want to wait until my last days to tell the truth.'

A wrap party was held at the end of the shoot in France, and the venue was the set upon which Leonardo had pretended to have his leg amputated. Leonardo was glad it was all over, not having enjoyed making the film nor having made the most of his stay in France. 'You know, it's such a cliché about the French, but it's the most true thing. I've never experienced in my life how rude these people are. Terrible,' he claimed.

It was at the wrap party that director Agnieszka Holland was able to assess her star actor, relating his abilities to those of Rimbaud and agreeing with Leonardo's father's speculation that his son's talents seemed to have an almost supernatural origin. 'He is the most surprising young actor,' she said of Leonardo. 'I think he's like a medium, it's not like a character. He opens his body and his mind to receive messages coming from another person's life. I think maybe Rimbaud was a medium, visited by extraterrestrials in a way, and this boy [Leonardo] has this capacity. After spending two months with him I don't know how he can know, but he's never wrong.'

'Death freaks me out. I don't know about an afterlife. I'm not religious, you know. I'm not an atheist, but I've never had a religion.'

The film did have a disappointing first run in the United States where it only grossed around $350,000. *Total Eclipse*, for all its high ambitions, was the first financial and critical flop on Leonardo's ever-growing resume. 'I think the only people who liked *Total Eclipse* were people who liked Rimbaud,' said Leonardo after the film had flopped. 'I don't know what to say about [it]. In the United States people don't really know who he is. I think maybe the film didn't explain enough.'

In keeping with his varied choices, Leonardo made use of his time in France to make what he dubbed as a 'furtive and friendly appearance' in the little-seen *Les Cent et une Nuits* (*101 Nights*), a French movie about the history of cinema directed by Agnes Varda, wife of French film-maker Jacques Demy.

A meditation on the centenary of cinema, the film sees 100-year-old Monsieur Cinema paid a visit by several notable movie stars – among them Leonardo's *Total Eclipse* co-star Romane Bohringer (she played Verlaine's long-suffering wife), his *This Boy's Life* and *Marvin's Room* co-star Robert DeNiro, Catherine Deneuve, Gerard Depardieu (whom he would later work with in *The Man In The Iron Mask*), his contemporary Stephen Dorff, Harrison Ford, Daryl Hannah, Emily Lloyd and Martin Sheen. Like the earlier short *The Foot Shooting Party*, *Les Cent Et Une Nuits* was to be another bizarre little blip on Leonardo's filmography, a bit of variety which kept his acting juices flowing.

A visit to Italy was next on Leonardo's European agenda. He travelled to Milan where he was invited by fashion designer Giorgio Armani to attend his latest fashion show. Staying in the Principe Hotel, Leonardo was glad of the chance to indulge what had become something of a hobby for him. He'd begun to visit as many fashion shows in the United States and Europe as he could – although whether the attraction was the clothes or the models was hard to tell. Stories of Leonardo's juvenile high jinks were not far behind his arrival in Milan, as staff reported sightings of the actor rollerblading naked along the hotel corridors at 6am, frightening the other guests. Leonardo denied the stories, claiming the phantom rollerblader was a friend, one of his entourage, whom he knew was wearing underwear at the time.

In the summer of 1996, Leonardo DiCaprio's short life nearly came to a violent and premature end – an event which would have bestowed upon him the gone-before-his-time James Dean-style aura that had been feared by some.

Leonardo and ten friends went skydiving over the Californian desert, jumping from 12,000ft, each in tandem with an instructor. Upon reaching 5,000ft they were to pull their rip cords and float gently to earth. When it came to Leonardo's turn, he found himself in mid-air mortal danger.

'That was scary,' recalled Leonardo once he was firmly back on terra firma. 'I had a guy on my back who pulled the cord for me and when it didn't open, he cut off the first parachute. It floated away and we started free-falling again, and I started freaking out. Then he managed to pull the second parachute and he steered us down. It was crazy.'

This brush with death didn't stop Leonardo pursuing dangerous sports. 'I like doing things that scare me. I went bungee jumping, but skydiving is just the sickest thing. The weird thing is, I wasn't shocked or paralysed by fear. I was more depressed than anything, sitting there really bummed out because I was the only guy out of all my friends to have his chute not open.'

Despite his cavalier approach to his own mortality, Leonardo did take some serious lessons from his mid-air freak-out. 'I made a little video afterwards, where I look into the camera all jittery and go, "Leonardo, if you're watching this, this is your last time skydiving. It's your first life-and-death experience. I want you to learn something from it."'

The near-death encounter revealed to Leonardo that his young life could be threatened by more than just the old Hollywood staples of a drugs overdose or a fatal car crash. 'Death freaks me out,' admitted Leonardo. 'I don't know about an afterlife. I'm not religious, you know. I'm not an atheist, but I've never had a religion. Some people that I know that I completely trust tell me stuff about ghosts and the afterlife that I can't argue with. My cousin saw his dead father's face in front of him: he woke up, closed his eyes, smacked himself, and still saw his father sitting there. There's got to be something else.'

Leonardo may have escaped James Dean-like notoriety through an early death, but the James Dean connection was one to haunt the young actor, with several Dean projects trying to tie Leonardo down to taking the starring role. Leonardo had his reservations about tackling the subject, even though biopics, from *This Boy's Life* and *The Basketball Diaries* to *Total Eclipse*, had been a feature of his career and provided some of his most challenging roles. 'If the right director gets involved, we'll see. The script is excellent, but I really don't know whether it would be the right thing for me to do. He's just such a colourful character to get into. At the same time, I could never really be him, he was such an original and I'd just be imitating him. I'm interested in James Dean, just for the fact that he could be such a damn challenge.' He was only the latest in a long line of young actors, among them Johnny Depp and Brad Pitt, to have turned down the role.

'I like doing things that scare me. I went bungee jumping, but skydiving is just the sickest thing.'

Leonardo doesn't even see himself as a Dean-like actor. 'I don't believe any of it,' he said of the hype surrounding him as a hot, young actor. 'I think about acting and the business all the time, that's the truth, about the roles, about whatever people are doing, what to do next, but as far as what people are saying about me . . . once in a blue moon I really think about it, you know, I really sit down and say, "Hey, is that true?" But it just doesn't register, because I read the stuff about me and it's not who I am. It's a cliché, but it's like they're writing about this guy that I've been made out to be.'

Despite his views, Leonardo shares much in common with James Dean, especially his sexually ambivalent aura on screen, which allows him to be attractive to both men and women. Critics, reviewing his performance in *The Quick And The Dead* had noted that he sometimes seemed more beautiful than his co-star Sharon Stone. Like such actors as Brad Pitt, Keanu Reeves and Johnny Depp, this sexual ambivalence has led to Leonardo becoming something of a gay icon, despite his own revulsion at gay sex as displayed during the making of *Total Eclipse*. 'No way,' responded Leonardo when the suggestion was made, betraying more of his nervousness surrounding homosexuality. 'That's just stuff. People may write that; it's not true. I mean, I've never put myself in that position.'

The position that Leonardo DiCaprio found himself in after eight feature films ranging from his early efforts in B-movie fodder to performance-centred contemporary drama like *What's Eating Gilbert Grape?* and *The Basketball Diaries* was one to be envied by many other actors. Oscar-nominated at a young age, Leonardo now had his pick of the parts for young actors in Hollywood. The one he chose next was to be a radical, new, funky interpretation of a classic role.

Post-Modern Romeo

*'There's some of Romeo's romance in me . . .
I romanticise a lot of things in my mind.'*
Leonardo DiCaprio

Now in his early twenties, Leonardo DiCaprio is the toast of Hollywood, a young actor of extraordinary power who has shown he can hold his own against more mature, more experienced actors. Often called 'the greatest actor of his generation' Leonardo has a lot to live up to after a mere handful of films, many of them critical hits but very few commercial successes. His most successful film managed the difficult task of being both – as well as providing Leonardo with the opportunity to put a unique spin on a classic character.

Before he jumped into *William Shakespeare's Romeo & Juliet*, however, the chance to work again opposite Robert DeNiro drew Leonardo to *Marvin's Room*, even though the part he was to play would mean him returning to playing a troubled teenager, as he had previously in *This Boy's Life*, *What's Eating Gilbert Grape?*, *The Quick And The Dead* and *The Basketball Diaries*. It was the strength of his co-stars – not only DeNiro, but Meryl Streep and Diane Keaton – which persuaded Leonardo to take the role.

Marvin's Room made its stage debut in New York in 1991, and won a great deal of acclaim for author Scott McPherson who'd based much of this work of fiction on events and people

'I've just got to maintain my passion for what I do.'

from his own life. The film based on the play tells the story of two sisters, the fiercely independent Lee (Meryl Streep) and her stay-at-home older sister Bessie (Diane Keaton). When Lee's troubled son Hank (Leonardo) burns down their home, she and his brother Charlie (Hal Scardino) head for Florida to stay with Bessie, who has her own troubles. She has spent many years looking after her bed-ridden father Marvin (Hume Cronyn) – a character never actually seen in the stage play – and his eccentric sister Ruth (Gwen Verdon), and has been diagnosed with leukaemia by Dr Wally (Robert DeNiro).

Leonardo recalled first coming across the *Marvin's Room* script when he was given a copy by his 'acting mentor' Robert DeNiro shortly after the pair had made *This Boy's Life*. 'I told him, "Whenever you get it assembled, let me know, and I'll do it." When I first read the script, I said: "Is this actually a movie?" I couldn't believe the way the dialogue occurred. It was unlike anything I'd ever read. The jokes just played as natural as possible, completely in conversation.'

With DeNiro and DiCaprio on board, *Marvin's Room* director Jerry Zaks had to fill the two leading female roles. Like DeNiro, Meryl Streep had long been interested in the material, and was offered the role of either sister, opting for the spunky part of Lee, on the proviso that Diane Keaton was offered the role of Bessie. Keaton soon agreed, and the cast was set. Between them, the *Marvin's Room* cast had secured nineteen Oscar nominations, with five wins.

Leonardo was part of an ensemble cast, almost a chance to relax before taking a taxing starring role in *Romeo & Juliet*, and so was able to bury himself in the role without worrying about the larger concerns of the film. He was playing another teenager with mental health problems, as in *What's Eating Gilbert Grape?*, but Hank was not simply another Arnie, being more than merely a chance for Leonardo to repeat a past success. 'The weird thing about Hank,' said Leonardo, 'is that he can never just go full force with something. He tries to open up to somebody like Bessie, and then something happens that sets him off, and they've got to go back to the start again.'

'I hate it . . . I feel that when I see myself and these other cute faces, I'm just part of this meat factory.'

Much of Leonardo's screen time was spent with Diane Keaton as Bessie, and she thoroughly enjoyed working with the young actor, impressed with his abilities. 'I think Bessie connects with Hank because seeing him is like seeing the beginning of life, seeing possibility and potential,' said Keaton. 'Bessie is thinking, "Look what's up ahead. What could happen, what he could do. I want this for him. He has all of this before him and it's going away from me. I'm leaving and he's starting." I think Bessie falls in love with Hank, in a way. And of course, when you think of Leonardo DiCaprio playing the part – what an amazing gift he has. And he's what? 22?'

Although she has lived with three of Hollywood's legendary leading men in her time, 51-year old Diane Keaton was more than smitten with young Leonardo during the shooting of *Marvin's Room*. She may have been the paramour of Warren Beatty, Al Pacino and Woody Allen at different points during her life, but it was Leonardo – 30 years her junior – who caught her attention.

'I was in love with him,' confessed Keaton about her infatuation with Leonardo. 'He's great, he's beautiful: that guy has really got it. So talented, so gifted and funny – everything you want in a person. He's like a light – he walks in and it's like magic. Meryl Streep and I would sit there and go: "God, this kid is so beautiful."'

While Keaton was infatuated with Leonardo, he took a different approach to her. 'He used to make fun of me,' she admitted. 'He did nothing but make fun of me. He made me feel like such a jerk. But I loved him. I was in love with him. Sure, I'll confess.'

Despite Keaton's keenness on him, it seems that Leonardo was more taken with Meryl Streep: 'Meryl Streep does things I would never have thought possible. She says her lines with such intensity on the set, and it comes out so naturally that the result is simply incredible on the big screen! Her presence on screen is outstanding. She was more than impressing to my eyes! In addition, she's an adorable woman.'

The obsession with Leonardo displayed by Diane Keaton was not peculiar to her. Leonardo was the subject of fantasies by many women – young and old – the world over, based on his film appearances and his off-screen persona. The perception of him as a sex symbol was not something which Leonardo appreciated. 'I hate it,' he has said of the fact that he's often portrayed as a movie hunk. 'I feel that when I see myself and these other cute faces, I'm just part of this meat factory. "Wow! Here's the hunk of the month! This month we're shoving down your throat this cute little kid – Oh, look! It's Leonardo DiCaprio! Isn't he cute! Let's put him on the cover and we'll sell more magazines!" That's definitely not what I want to be and I've tried hard to get away from that whole situation. Just being in there annoys me. It gives me a yucky feeling.' It was a long way from his early days as the TV soap pin-up of the month, when Leonardo and his mother Irmelin would conspire with the TV magazines to concoct good PR stories about the rising actor.

A soap-opera style emotional drama, *Marvin's Room* relied on the quality of the performances and the deftness of the script to make its impact 'The actors in this cast,' said director Jerry Zaks of his stars, including Leonardo, 'are capable of going to that emotional place where these characters have to get to make this story believable and affecting. They're also capable of great comedy and great depth.'

Leonardo DiCaprio had a dream role waiting just around the corner. The film was destined to have a huge impact, but when Leonardo first heard of the interest in him for the lead role in a new version of *William Shakespeare's Romeo & Juliet*, he was less than impressed. 'I wasn't sure at first – I didn't want to run around in tights, swinging a sword. I was given a script and at the time I didn't really want to do a traditional version of *Romeo And Juliet*. I wouldn't have done it if it had been a period piece. It has been done so many times, and so many people loved the Zeffirelli film. But what Baz [Luhrmann, the director] had done was reinvent it, and in the process he discovered new ways of treating the play and the characters.'

Further investigation opened Leonardo's eyes to the uniqueness of this project. Baz Luhrmann, the director of the film, was an Australian who'd been previously acclaimed for *Strictly Ballroom*, persuaded Leonardo and his father George to come 'down under' to find out more about the radical take he was proposing for this modern version of the classic tale.

Leonardo's father had been instrumental in his script choices since his career began several years before, but it was with *Romeo & Juliet* that George's recommendation caused an initially reluctant Leonardo to take a second look at the project. 'He filters the crappy scripts out,' said Leonardo of George's role in his career. 'He recommends the ones he thinks I should take a look at. He's the person I most look up to in this world, he's the most intelligent guy I've ever met, so naturally I respect his opinion more than anybody's. He's the man.'

The pair took a trip to meet Luhrmann and listen to his pitch for a faithful but dramatically different version of Shakespeare's tale. 'I was curious, so I went out to Australia to do a workshop with him [Luhrmann]

> 'Leo's brilliant . . . It was a real treat working with him.' Claire Danes on Leonardo.

and he told me about the new ideas he wanted to bring to the movie and then I became interested. I stayed there for two weeks. And then I realised how magical, energetic, and electric he wanted his adaptation to be,' recalled Leonardo of this 1995 trip, two years before the film was released. 'What was crucial to me was that this was going to be a genuine *Romeo & Juliet*, the real thing – not another *West Side Story*. Instead of the swords and a lot of elaborate costumes, [Luhrmann] wanted to bring to the movie a lot of religious themes, the cars, the guns.'

'I was in love with him.' Diane Keaton on Leonardo.

In Marvin's Room *it was the strength of his co-stars, Diane Keaton and Meryl Streep which persuaded Leonardo to take the role.*

'Meryl Streep does things I would never have thought possible . . .
Her presence on screen is outstanding.'

It wasn't easy persuading American studios more used to high-concept, easily accessible adventure films with big name stars and lots of explosions to mount a new production of a work by an Elizabethan playwright not known for his simple-to-follow plots and marketable gimmicks. 'The history of the film is a big "No" from the studio's point of view,' explained Luhrmann. 'When I said I wanted to do Shakespeare, they said "No". So I went off, saw a picture of Leonardo, and thought "This guy looks like Romeo." Then I heard he was up for the Academy Award and thought "This guy must be able to act, too."'

'The created world really helped me as an actor. It heightened everything, which made it more dangerous, more interesting and more liberating.'

Luhrmann realised he'd made a lucky discovery in latching on to Leonardo for the part of Romeo. 'I thought that Leonardo was an extraordinary young actor, and I thought he'd make a great Romeo. It's important to reveal these eternal characters anew for every generation, and Leo is particularly suited for this. He does seem to symbolise his generation. I just thought he'd be a perfect Romeo: it was as simple as that,' said Luhrmann of his inspired casting choice.

During a second trip to Australia, Luhrmann videotaped the acting workshop he carried out with Leonardo, intending to use the footage to convince both himself and the studio that Leonardo would work in the lead role, and to show something of the intended style of the film. A series of actresses-for-hire stood in for the part of Juliet opposite Leonardo. Eventually, the director was able to persuade 20th Century Fox that his proposed version of the oft-told tale would draw a young audience. 'The studio said: "Oh, we get it, it's about gangs. Gangs are good. And they take their clothes off?" And I said, "Well yeah, Romeo and Juliet have sex and everything . . .".'

To begin with, Leonardo was as phased by Luhrmann's ideas about the film as the studio executives had been. 'I wasn't sure how it would all work out,' he admitted, when faced with the screenplay. 'I have to say that the first time I really knew it was working was the first day of work. It actually seemed more natural, more "meant to be" than a traditional version. Baz immersed us in this *Romeo & Juliet* world, so the whole experience from those first readings and rehearsals in Australia to the end of shooting was like going to Shakespeare Camp.'

In common with many American film actors who tackle Shakespeare, Leonardo felt somewhat daunted at the prospect of capturing the language. 'At first I thought I would have to put on an English accent and try a sort of affected Shakespeare thing. But Baz explained he wanted to make it understandable, very clear, and after working with him a while, I began to feel more comfortable with it. I had a lot of fears about speaking the language at first, because I'm not classically trained. But Baz wanted it to sound conversational – he told us to play around with it. I'd never done much Shakespeare in school and it was kinda frightening to read through. Then I saw Keanu Reeves in *Much Ado About Nothing* and I knew if he can do it, I can do it too . . .'

Getting into Romeo's skin was a slow process for Leonardo, who had never faced the challenge of playing such a fantasy figure in a fantasy world before. 'I understood the character. There's some of Romeo's romance in me, I think. I romanticise a lot of things in my mind. It took a while to get accustomed to it. With each character I do, I like to get everything done from the start and then know what I'm doing throughout the whole thing and learn as I go along. I'm never really like the ultimate method man who has to compile everything and be that character all the time. I sort of see how it goes as it goes along. I just had to be prepared for the emotional points that Romeo goes through because he's not a light-hearted guy, he has to go through some heavy stuff.'

Finding a Juliet to team up with Leonardo's modern Romeo was the next task he and Luhrmann faced. After a search that included auditions by Leonardo's friend Alicia Silverstone, Liv Tyler and rising actress Natalie Portman, it was Leonardo who was instrumental in casting young actress Claire Danes. 'I saw her television show, *My So Called Life*, and I knew from that point on that she was an extremely intense emotional girl and possessed a lot of the stuff that we wanted Juliet to be,' claimed Leonardo. 'I told the director about her. I knew she'd be the one. Other actresses came in with a flowery version of Juliet. We didn't want a flowery, over-dramatic version of Juliet, but somebody that was really forceful, because she actually laid down the law to Romeo.'

'I've never been a Romeo who meets a girl and falls for her immediately ... It's been a much slower process for me each time I've gone into a relationship.'

Both Leonardo and Danes claimed that working together helped them to develop and discover the hearts of their romantic characters. 'Leo is brilliant,' said Danes of her co-star. 'It's been thrilling to work with him. He's one of the most interesting people I've ever met and he is a very open, honest and true actor. He is also extremely funny. Sometimes I'd be doubled over in pain from laughing so hard, and that's important, sometimes, especially when the scenes are intense. It was a real treat working with him.'

Production took place in and around Mexico City, from Churubusco Studios to the barren lands of Texcoco, from the famed Chapultepec Castle to the beaches of Veracruz. All the location work was combined to make up the mythical world of Verona Beach. *Romeo & Juliet* was not a trouble-free production, with many of the problems that occurred being down to the film's Mexican location. A 90 mile-per-hour sand storm blew up, halting filming on the beach and knocking down standing sets. It was followed by a series of attacks from killer bees, multiple broken legs and even a serious bout of food poisoning which closed down the production for four days.

'We were waiting for the locusts,' jokes Danes, who felt there was already enough to challenge her in just playing a modern Juliet without extra distraction. 'There was no simple, pleasant scene where I'm talking to my best friend over coffee. It was, like, I'm being disowned by my father or I'm about to kill myself.' She also had to cope with Leonardo's practical jokes on set, which served to irritate the rather serious actress. She regarded Leonardo's antics as juvenile and soon tensions arose between the pair. 'There were arguments,' said Luhrmann. 'Sometimes they were like two kids on holiday and sometimes it was like you were dragging your children through a desert and they were starving and suffering. But because they were so young and in the middle of such extraordinary events, I think they came to rely on each other, which was a great thing to behold.'

Leonardo's practical jokes were not taken so seriously by other members of the cast, and even the director himself was a target. John Leguizamo, the actor playing Tybalt, was a victim of Leonardo's penchant for imitating his co-stars: 'I'd walk in

'I wasn't sure at first – I didn't want to run around in tights, swinging a sword.'

Action was one of the components director Baz Luhrmann brought to his version of Romeo & Juliet.

front of the camera, and Leonardo would do my lines all screechy, "Thou or I must go!" So the next time I'd become really self-conscious. I just hated him, because it came so easy to that little blond, happy, golden-boy. He'd smoke a cigarette, do some laps, do Michael Jackson, go on the set and there it was.'

Even director Baz Luhrmann didn't escape Leonardo's impersonations. 'People say that Marlon Brando was a constant practical joker,' noted Luhrmann, 'and you might see 30 characters come out of Leonardo in a day. A regular sport with Leonardo is to impersonate me in a fairly cruel and uncompromising way. But acting is playing, and all that fooling around is keeping him in a constant state of play.'

The locations in Mexico suited Leonardo, but he found some of the harrowing scenes hard to pin down. 'It's not really easy to be in Mexico, but it's very close to LA so I could drive home whenever I wanted to. There were a lot of weird things going on. People wanted money and there were kidnappings. We all got sick and needed weeks off to recover, but the chaos in Mexico City fuelled the actors. We were so crazed about what we were hearing every day, about people getting killed in our hotel and whatnot, that it gave us some incentive to our parts. The Tybalt death scene was hard. I had to sit there all night with this big fan blowing wind at me, and the rain was coming down. I was sitting there with hardly anything on, screaming "Juliet" three hundred times. I've been in the water so much, it's like an aquatic version of *Romeo & Juliet*. It was a rough movie.'

The thing that served to capture the imagination of the actors on the film, as well as critics and audiences when it was released, was the magical, mythical, fantasy world in which Luhrmann had decided to set his take on the tale. 'The idea behind "the created world"', he explained, 'was that it's a made-up world comprised of 20th century icons, and these images are there to clarify what's being said, because once you understand it the power and beauty of the language works its magic on you. The idea was to find icons that everybody comprehends, that are overtly clear. The hope was that by associating the characters and places with those images, the language would be freed from its cage of obscurity.'

That meant a radical departure for this *Romeo And Juliet* from what had gone before, both on film and on stage. Luhrmann's vision resulted in Leonardo playing Romeo as a James Dean figure, Danes' Juliet as a hip, modern young woman who knows her own mind, Tybalt (John Leguizamo) becomes a deranged headcase, while Mercutio (Harold Perrineau) is a cross-dressing, drug-taking, camp diva. It was enough to have the Bard spinning in his grave – and to bring an outcry from Shakespeare purists.

For Leonardo, these developments from the original play were vital. 'The created world really helped me as an actor. It heightened everything, which made it more dangerous, more interesting and more liberating. It gave me more freedom to try different things with the character and the scene, because we were not held down by the traditional rules.'

Packed with visual trickery – hence the shorthand notion that this is MTV Shakespeare – this *Romeo And Juliet* is set in a modern fantasy world, in which Shakespeare's Verona becomes Luhrmann's Verona Beach, a community based on Florida's exotic Miami. Inhabited by powerful families whose children form gangs, where guns and cars replace swords and horses, where local landmarks include the Globe Pool Hall, the Shylock Bank and the Out Damn Spot Dry Cleaners, it's a witty, visual, rousing and moving experience, in which the actors bring their characters to life in a way which connects with a contemporary audience, despite the difficulty such audiences normally have with the Elizabethan language. 'In fact, what we've done,' admitted Luhrmann, 'is set the film in the world of the movies. None of it particularly adds up, chronologically. Some of it looks like it's from the seventies, some from the forties. Stylistically, it changes very dramatically, echoing film genres, from *Rebel Without A Cause* to the Busby Berkeley musicals, or a Clint Eastwood Dirty Harry picture.'

'At first I thought I would have to put on an English accent and try a sort of affected Shakespeare thing.'

At the heart of this assured and ground-breaking film is the romance between Leonardo and Danes, and it was this, almost as much as the superficial style and visual jokes, that truly grabbed audiences worldwide, turning *Romeo & Juliet* into an international phenomenon and thrusting Leonardo onto the A-list of Hollywood stars. Romeo was the role which finally brought Leonardo's off-screen life as a teen pin-up and youth icon to life on the big screen where he wasn't playing a troubled teenager responsible to others. Romeo's actions break the taboos of Verona Beach, but he is wilfully responsible to no one but himself and his one true love – Juliet.

Opening on 1 November 1996, the film had taken $36 million in its first month, which included a stay at the number one spot, and soon passed the $50 million mark. That performance, before the video release, was not bad for the film which had a 72-day shoot and a mere $15 million budget.

With *William Shakespeare's Romeo & Juliet* a rip-roaring success world-wide, privacy became ever harder to come by for Leonardo, and the pressure to meet his

'What was crucial to me was that this was going to be a genuine Romeo And Juliet not another West Side Story.'

fans demands increased to ridiculous levels. When playing basketball with friends, Leonardo found himself caught up in a bizarre memorabilia scam. 'This girl came up and said: "I'm your biggest fan. Give me your T-shirt." I told her: "I'm not giving you this T-shirt off my back, I'm playing basketball. I'll give you an autograph or something, but that's about it." Ten minutes later she gets her mother to come and tell me she has a daughter dying of cancer in a hospital and that I should sign my T-shirt to her. So, trying to be a nice guy, I did.' As the woman disappeared around the corner, Leonardo remembered the conversation had started off as a car crash victim, not cancer, so he gave chase and found the woman and her daughter around the corner laughing about duping Leonardo DiCaprio. 'It really bummed me out,' recalled Leonardo of the incident. 'It's like I'm not even there, like I'm just some mechanical thing walking around that isn't really human. I took it really personally.'

Following the American release of *William Shakespeare's Romeo & Juliet*, controversy erupted around Leonardo DiCaprio in early March 1997 when publications around the world accused him and Demi Moore, Hollywood's highest paid actress, of enjoying an illicit tryst behind the back of Moore's husband, superstar Bruce Willis.

Moore's penchant for losing her clothing in her movies, a habit which culminated in her $12 million payday for getting naked in the flop *Striptease*, paired with Leonardo's hot performance in *Romeo & Juliet* were the elements the headline writers needed. Newspapers splashed their front pages with huge, lurid headlines such as 'Demi's Secret Night With Movie Romeo'. One ran 'Strip Beauty Demi Takes Hunk Home' above pages of blurry photographs showing Moore – shaven-headed for her

role in *GI Jane* – and Leonardo enjoying coffee in the Koo-Koo-Roo chicken restaurant on Sunset Boulevard in Los Angeles, and returning to her 'idyllic seafront mansion' in Malibu. The newspapers claimed that Leonardo did not leave Demi's home until the following morning. Bruce Willis, meanwhile, was 3,000 miles away filming a remake of *The Day of the Jackal* in Delaware, while their three daughters were with their nanny in Idaho.

In astonishing detail, reporter Stuart White, writing in Britain's *News Of The World* Sunday newspaper, chronicled what the paper claimed was an 'amazing date'. White followed Moore and Leonardo from their meeting on Sunset Boulevard to her mansion, where they had pizza delivered at 10pm. Leonardo allegedly answered the door and collected the pizza. White further alleged that Leonardo left the following morning: 'Leonardo emerged, still wearing the same clothes he was wearing the night before.'

The reports – picked up and repeated in newspapers and magazines around the world – caused an immediate storm and had Demi Moore threatening various publications with law suits. A spokesman for 34-year-old Moore denied that 22-year-old Leonardo had spent the night, claiming he was just one among many guests attending a movie screening. 'Leonardo is like a younger brother to Demi,' claimed the spokesperson. 'He is a friend of Demi and Bruce. He did not stay overnight. Demi had a series of meetings with people all day. One of those was Leonardo. They discussed a project. Other people were there and it wasn't a long meeting. Then Leonardo left. Demi's not smitten with him.'

'I am friends with Demi. Don't believe everything you read.'

That seemed to kill the story, except that those surrounding both Demi Moore and Leonardo continued to make claims about the pair. Friends of Demi Moore claimed the actress had become infatuated with the young actor after seeing him in *Romeo & Juliet*, and was desperate to make a movie with him. Another colleague claimed that Moore was developing a film project which called for a relationship between an older woman and a younger man – and she has Leonardo firmly in mind. 'She wanted to meet Leonardo to see if they had any chemistry together,' claimed the anonymous source to the *News Of The World*. 'I'm anxious to see how Bruce is going to handle this. I'd hate to see an altercation.' The row did not seem to phase Leonardo. 'I am friends with Demi. Don't believe everything you read,' he simply stated.

Leonardo had the perfect answer to claims of a secret relationship with Demi Moore – his girlfriend of a year, model Kristen Zang. 'This is my first long-term relationship,' he said, 'and I can't wait to see her at the end of the day. She's the cutest girl in the world.' His years of hanging around fashion shows had finally paid off, and Leonardo was now able to attend the shows with a model on his arm.

The pair attended the premiere of *Romeo & Juliet* together, and in the spring of 1997 Leonardo finally moved out of the home he'd shared with his mother in Los Angeles to set up home with Zang. 'I've never been a Romeo who meets a girl and falls for her immediately,' he said, revealing his cautious nature when it comes to affairs of the heart – a factor which makes an illicit liaison with Demi Moore even more unlikely. 'It's been a much slower process for me each time I've gone into a relationship.'

Despite much speculation Leonardo had not been firmly linked with any girlfriends, until Zang, other than the erroneous reports of a liaison with Alicia Silverstone. Gossip columns had been full of Leonardo partying in New York during the shooting of *The*

Basketball Diaries, including trips out on the town with actress Juliette Lewis, Brad Pitt's ex and his co-star in *The Basketball Diaries*, as well as Ralph Lauren model Bridget Hall. Although often linked with his co-stars, such as Claire Danes in *Romeo & Juliet* and Kate Winslet in *Titanic*, Leonardo didn't believe dating co-stars was a good idea. 'It's like taking your job home. I prefer ordinary girls – you know, college students, waitresses, that sort of thing. Most of the girls I go out with are just good friends. Just because I go out to the cinema with a girl, it doesn't mean we are dating.'

Out-of-the-ordinary model Kristen Zang had changed all that for Leonardo. 'Love at first sight hasn't happened to me yet, but I do believe it can happen. I have done some romantic things in my time. I flew [Kristen] down to Mexico to visit me on location [for *Titanic*].'

Never one to talk to the press – he distrusts journalists and the media in general and is constantly late for pre-arranged interviews – Leonardo was surprisingly happy to discuss his relationship with Zang, as if it would stop them prying into other aspects of his life. 'We've been going out for about a year. We're pretty happy. What attracted me to her at first was that she's good looking, and that's why I started talking to her. I thought she was cute – like the cutest thing I'd ever seen in my life!'

New to the romance game, Leonardo set out to enjoy himself, claiming that Zang brought him some peace and an escape from the hurly-burly of the movie world. 'She's really sweet – and she calms me down. She's easy going about everything, and not high-strung, which I would not be able to deal with.'

The clichés of romance did not come easy to young Leonardo and neither did thoughts of making a long term commitment through marriage. After all, playing Romeo was just a part. 'I've never really been that type. With Romeo and Juliet, you're talking about two people who meet one night, and get married the same night. I believe in love at first sight – but it hasn't happened to me yet. I've bought Kristen a watch and flowers and things, but I haven't climbed up a building or anything like that. I don't know if I'm ever getting married. I'm probably not going to get married unless I live with somebody for 10 or 20 years. But these people [Romeo and Juliet] took a chance and they did it. We don't have the balls that Romeo did,' admitted Leonardo. Despite rumours late in 1997 that he and Zang were a thing of the past, Leonardo continued to talk about her in interviews.

'I prefer ordinary girls – you know, college students, waitresses, that sort of thing. Most of the girls I go out with are just good friends. Just because I go out to the cinema with a girl, it doesn't mean we are dating.'

For someone enjoying the success that Leonardo DiCaprio had, to sign up for a journey on board a cinematic version of the sinking of the ill-fated Titanic may have seemed like a foolhardy move, given the history of the vehicle and the films made about it. However, despite the delays and problems that awaited Leonardo during production, James Cameron's epic film about the sinking of the unsinkable ship had the potential to be not only an Oscar-winner, but also a blockbuster, and Leonardo didn't want to miss his opportunity.

The Titanic was something of an obsession of mega-budget blockbuster director James Cameron. From the original 1985 low budget *Terminator* movie starring

'There's some of Romeo's romance in me, I think. I romanticise a lot of things in my mind.'

A match made in heaven – Leonardo as Romeo and Claire Danes as Juliet.

'Then I saw Keanu Reeves in *Much Ado About Nothing* and I knew if he can do it, I can do it too . . .'

Arnold Schwarzenegger, Cameron had graduated to bigger budget, special-effects-laden epics like *Aliens, Terminator 2: Judgement Day* and the waterlogged adventure flop *The Abyss*. Despite his production problems during *The Abyss*, as well as it's poor critical and commercial reception, Cameron was tempted back into the water for *Titanic*. It proved, once again, to be a bad choice.

Interest in the story was not limited to James Cameron. It was the continuing public fascination with the tale that led him and two studios – Fox and Paramount – to gamble on the project as a blockbuster film, aiming for release on 4th July 1997, the peak of the summer movie season.

The original, 'unsinkable' Titanic had been built between 1910 and 1912 at a cost of $7.3 million, the grandest ship of its age. Five days into its maiden voyage, the ship sank on 14th April 1912 after striking an iceberg 400 miles off the coast of Newfoundland. Around 1520 people died, with just 700 or so surviving. Almost immediately, the tragic tale inspired film recreations, the most notorious of which was Lord Grade's seventies disaster *Raise The Titanic* – the failure of which led the irrepressible impresario to quip, 'It would have been cheaper to lower the Atlantic.'

'It was closer to manual labour than shooting a film. I always think of something Michael Caton-Jones told me: "Pain is temporary. Film is forever." '

As James Cameron prepared to shoot his movie, Broadway was also taken with the Titanic as a theatre production the $10 million musical won a Tony award and broke box-office records at the Lunt-Fontanne Theatre. Documentaries, over 100 books, CD Roms and internet sites continue to 'celebrate' the sinking of the 'unsinkable' ship.

Offered the lead role in *Titanic*, Leonardo DiCaprio was faced with something of a dilemma. He couldn't play the teen characters of *Marvin's Room* and *What's Eating Gilbert Grape?* forever. At 22 he could still pass for seventeen, as *Marvin's Room* showed, but his 'little boy dazed' routine had been seen once too often by audiences. He had to secure leading man status and start playing characters of more responsibility, in line with his own age. *Romeo & Juliet* had given Leonardo his first shot at a leading role, where he had carried much of the film. 'It's my first sort of commercial attempt, but it made sense for me because I'm not that kind of guy and I'm not going to continue to do that kind of movie,' he said as he prepared for a gruelling seven month filming process. Cast alongside Leonardo was Kate Winslet, a rising British actress, who'd featured in an acclaimed adaptation of Thomas Hardy's *Jude* and alongside Emma Thompson in *Sense And Sensibility*.

Following *Romeo & Juliet*, the romance of the story in *Titanic* caught Leonardo's attention. 'It was the only one that really had a good story to it and had some real, emotionally-charged characters and wasn't me playing some sort of cyborg,' he said of his venture into the world of blockbusters. 'It was something that I probably would have done if it was commercial or not, and that's the way I choose movies. It's a love story – lower class artist meets upper class girl and then falling in love and defying what's going on in their society and their world – then, all of a sudden, it all goes down. I'm this poor young artist from Paris, and Kate plays an upper class girl, but she's engaged to somebody else.'

In keeping with other James Cameron films, the production process for *Titanic* was an epic in itself. An almost-to-scale 750ft replica of the ship was constructed on the coast of Baja California, Mexico by 20th Century Fox, a construction visible from a mile along the beach. A fully-fledged movie studio was created on the site with three sound stages and production offices, all forty minutes from the Texan border. The tank in which the set was built held millions of gallons of water and every detail on the ship was painstakingly recreated. To stage the sinking of the ship, giant hydraulic pistons tipped the entire construction – a mechanical special effect which was to result in injuries for many members of the cast.

'The best thing about acting is that I get to lose myself in another character and actually get paid for it . . . It's a great outlet. I'm not really sure who I am – it seems I change every day.'

As if the scale of the production was not enough, things took a bizarre turn when a disgruntled member of the production crew, allegedly a chef, spiked the crew's clam chowder with PCP, a hallucinogenic drug also known as angel dust, resulting in several lost days of production and an outbreak of illness among cast and crew alike. Fifty people were taken to hospital in Nova Scotia, officially said to be victims of 'food poisoning'. Bill Paxton, who plays a maritime salvage expert in the contemporary framing story in *Titanic*, said: 'Some people were laughing, some crying, some throwing up. One minute I felt okay, then I felt so goddamn anxious.'

A doctor from the local casualty unit noted: 'These people were stoned. They had no idea what was going on.' Also clueless were the police called in to investigate the mysterious incident. 'We're not even sure whether it was a prank or mistake,' admitted baffled police sergeant Richard Hollinshead. 'We're still investigating . . .'

Additionally, several extras were injured in two separate incidents. *Time* magazine reported in December 1996 that extras were rushed to a local hospital with broken ribs and sprained ankles. Worse was to come during the shooting of the climactic sinking scenes, including ten crew members having to undergo surgery after falling onto railings when the deck of the ship was titled to almost 90 degrees.

These incidents resulted in the Screen Actors Guild sending a representative to monitor the production process. Their man in Mexico was to 'investigate the working conditions . . . and to bring every possible pressure to bear on the producers to substantially and immediately improve matters.' However, the Guild found no evidence of lax safety standards. 'Jim will put himself in danger before anyone else,' said one member of the production team.

In February of 1997, it was Leonardo DiCaprio who was on the receiving end of one of *Titanic*'s many on-set accidents. The actor narrowly missed being crushed by a horse during the filming of a sequence, adding to the accident-prone nature of what James Cameron began calling 'the definitive disaster movie'. While shooting a storm scene, during which Leonardo and Kate Winslet were securely tied to the ship's railing, a real storm blew up, causing crew members to panic and flee from the set, leaving the starring actors attached to the rails for over an hour in the gusting winds. After they were rescued, Kate Winslet was so upset at the incident that filming was halted for the day. In common with complaints from actors and crew alike on Cameron's previous water borne epic *The Abyss*, those on *Titanic* nicknamed their control-obsessed, perfectionist director 'Captain Bligh'. An employee of Cameron's

'I'm probably not going to get married unless I live with somebody for 10 to 20 years. But these people [Romeo and Juliet] took a chance and they did it. We don't have the balls that Romeo did.'

production company Lightstorm Entertainment confirmed the director's temper tantrums. '[Jim] does shout a lot on set. He yells and yells until it's perfect. So the crew will have been definitely complaining about that.'

Although pencilled in for an Independence Day mid-summer release date, it was clear as footage came into Cameron's own Digital Domain computer effects house that the work that was needed would mean release prints would simply not be ready for that date. At the end of Spring 1997 Paramount Pictures began to warn cinemas unofficially that the movie would not be ready for its release date, suggesting that a November debut was a more likely prospect. Paramount Vice President Robert G. Friedman initially denied these reports when they appeared in *Variety*.

With principal photography complete and digital effects work underway, the budget had ballooned to $185–$200 million, making *Titanic* the most expensive film of all time, as Cameron's *Terminator 2* had been previously. 'No-one knows the exact figure,' admitted an on-set source, 'but they are talking about it breaking $200 million.' Digital Domain refused to take the blame for the delay, pointing the finger instead at Cameron's two months over-run on filming, with shooting finally wrapping in late March 1997. As the possible release dates slipped through July and into August, Cameron began farming special effects shots out to other effects houses, including his rivals at Industrial Light and Magic. It was a move that was interpreted as signs of panic on board the good ship *Titanic*. Finally, an official release date of December 19th was announced and some of the panic at the studios subsided.

'*Titanic*, even in its unfinished state, is spectacular,' said Robert G. Friedman, vice chairman of Paramount Pictures' Motion Picture Group, announcing the new release date. 'The decision to push it back was a difficult one which required us to compare the rising curve of compromises to the film against the descending curve of commercial gain in late summer. As both Paramount and 20th Century Fox believe strongly that the film can play well in any season, we elected to move out of an already crowded summer.'

Even with the positive buzz the director and studio tried to generate around *Titanic*, a film costing over $200 million would need to do business of about $500 million world-wide for any of the two studios involved to make money – and the previous year's blockbuster, *Mission Impossible,* a huge international success, had only grossed around $450 million world-wide.

'It's my first sort of commercial attempt, but it made sense for me because I'm not that kind of guy and I'm not going to continue to do that kind of movie.'

The filming of *Titanic* had been unlike any other movie Leonardo had ever been involved in. 'I've been doing smaller, more artistic films throughout my whole career. This was . . . quite an experience,' said Leonardo recalling the ups and downs of the seven month shoot. 'I have to say I probably won't do anything like it again. It was closer to manual labour than shooting a film. I always think of something Michael Caton-Jones told me: "Pain is temporary. Film is forever." And now it's over. Well, all respect to the people who do those sorts of movies, but it's not for me.'

Evidently unhappy with the way director James Cameron treated his actors like cattle, Leonardo felt disappointed that the love story which had initially drawn him to the project was now playing second fiddle to the effects, the overblown budget and the tales of trouble on the set. Even so – and ever the professional – Leonardo refused to badmouth either Cameron or his co-star Kate Winslet. 'We sort of prepared for what we would say if this question arose,' admitted Leonardo, laying bare the process of film promotion public relations in which the stars are not supposed to criticise each other but simply promote the film. 'My response is that Kate is a terrific, beautiful, great, talented girl.'

Despite evident enmity between the two stars on-set, somehow reports of a blossoming romance between Leonardo and Kate Winslet were soon hitting the papers. The young actor was quick to attempt to nip the stories in the bud, fearing a repeat of the Demi Moore controversy. 'We are just friends, there is no spark between us at all,' he said, loading his 'the kisses-were just-for-the-cameras' response with an implied criticism of his co-star and director for failing to provide the right signs of romance on screen in the finished film. Claims were made to the press that the pair of leading actors had become inseparable, eating romantic meals together, popping into each other's trailers and generally spending a lot of time together when not shooting. 'Kate had her eye on Leonardo from the word go,' said one source on the movie's set. 'He took some time to notice her, but Kate's a great laugh and it looks like she's charmed him.'

'It gets to the point of when you're hot, you're hot, and when you're not, you're not. It's so true. I have to slow down soon.'

Whether there was any romance off-screen for the pair – and they both deny it – those who read the script of *Titanic* claim to have made a severe dent in a box of tissues by the end, confirming the epic romance at the centre of the film which had so attracted Leonardo to the starring role. Even more positive were reports from those who viewed James Cameron's early cut of the film, claiming it was a sweeping, tragic romance on a par with David Lean's *Dr Zhivago*. Of course, these reports came from studio executives who had every reason to talk up the troubled production.

The pressure was certainly on when it came to *Titanic*, and Leonardo was driven to give the best performance he could, despite competing with the recreated spectacle of the ship, the special effects and working with a director who was more interested in co-ordinating an epic than directing his actors. Through it all, he had to perform. 'You really can't think about that when you're shooting, because if you do it's gonna make you one hundred times worse. I can see how it could be easily affected because I think about stuff like that all the time. It's a hard position to be in. Just because you may have done a good performance once doesn't mean you're always gonna be good. That's why you have some of the greatest actors in the world going a little bit nuts: "What happened? Do you still love me?" It's that type of situation and it's an easy trap to fall into.'

With the struggles of *Titanic* behind him, and before any critical fall-out or acclaim upon its release, Leonardo was back at work again, taking a central role in a new version of *The Man In The Iron Mask*. Tackling *Romeo & Juliet* had obviously given him a taste for costume drama. The film had been delayed due to the overruns on *Titanic*, and eventually got underway in Paris when Leonardo finally escaped from the doomed ship.

Adapted from the Alexander Dumas novel and directed by Randall Wallace, the Oscar-winning screenwriter for Mel Gibson's hack'n'slash Scottish epic *Braveheart*, *The Man In The Iron Mask* rounded up a host of star names to appear alongside Leonardo, who took the title role of King Louis. Gabriel Byrne was cast as D'Artagnan, with Gérard

Leonardo and girlfriend Kristen Zang enjoy the limelight at the premiere of Romeo & Juliet.

'This is my first long-term relationship . . . and I can't wait to see her at the end of the day. She's the cutest girl in the world.'

Depardieu as Porthos, Jeremy Irons as Aramis and John Malkovich as Athos. French actress and star of *Nikita* and *Innocent Blood* Anne Parillaud took the role of the Queen Mother, Anne of d'Autriche.

While shooting in early summer of 1997, Leonardo signed up for new projects, determined to make the most of his star status which had resulted from *Romeo & Juliet*. 'I don't care what people say about me,' he said of his heavy workload and worries that he might be watering down his performances. 'It gets to the point of when you're hot, you're hot, and when you're not, you're not. It's so true. I have to slow down soon.'

Films clamouring for Leonardo's involvement included a black and white drama called *Don's Plum* to be directed by R.D. Robb, featuring Amber Benson, Scott Bloom, Kevin Connelly, Jenny Lewis, and Tobey Maguire alongside Leonardo. The director of *Four Weddings and a Funeral* and *Donnie Brasco*, Mike Newell, wanted Leonardo to commit to his film *The Last Train For Memphis* based on the early days of Elvis Presley. Leonardo was to play the young Elvis, but given his reluctance to take on the role of James Dean, the likelihood of him playing Elvis seemed even more remote.

'If you can do what you do best and be happy, you're further along in life than most people.'

'I can't make all the films people say I'm doing,' said Leonardo, denying he was to feature alongside Sean Penn in his film about the Mitchell brothers, being too young to tackle the parts of Artie or Jim Mitchell. Indeed, the James Dean film was raised again as a possibility, with director Michael Mann (*Heat*) still pursuing the reluctant Leonardo: 'I don't think it's a good idea to take on the personality of another actor, particularly a legend.' One ambition he did express was a desire to work with director Danny Boyle, the man behind the surprise Scottish hit films *Shallow Grave* and *Trainspotting*.

Early in 1997, Leonardo signed on to star in the historical thriller *Slay The Dreamer*, based around the 1968 assassination of Dr Martin Luther King Jr. The script, by writers Mark Lane and Donald Freed, featured Jeffrey Jenkins (Leonardo), an ambitious young lawyer who is inadvertently drawn into a confrontation with his powerful father over the facts surrounding the assassination. 'The unique dramatic structure of the screenplay allows DiCaprio's fictional protagonist to intersect historical fact with startling results,' claimed producer Leonard Hill.

The screenplay for the film was based on an investigation into the assassination conducted by Rev. James Lawson, the then Memphis-based minister who led Dr King's school of non-violence, and attorney Mark Lane (who co-wrote the script) who represented the accused killer, James Earl Ray. 'Ray was never brought to trial and no jury has ever sifted through the tragic events of 4th April 1968,' said Hill. 'The sources uncovered by Lawson and Lane, combined with new information obtained through the Freedom of Information Act, have enabled the writers to construct a powerful and revelatory tale.'

Although financing was not in place for the film, with the producers intending to raise the money independent of the studio system, Leonardo committed himself to playing the part when filming began, scheduled for September 1997. 'Leonardo DiCaprio has shown himself to be an actor of extraordinary craft and exemplary courage,' said producer Nick Wechsler of the film's star name. 'DiCaprio's commitment will transform a remarkable script into an unforgettable film.' The producers hoped to persuade Samuel L. Jackson to co-star.

Leonardo DiCaprio has been a movie actor for less than a decade and he has already made a phenomenal impact. His performances have been the key to the critical acclaim dished out to a series of under-performing films. With the notable exception of *William Shakespeare's Romeo & Juliet*, none of Leonardo's movies have been big commercial hits – the kind of films which normally launch their stars to superstar status. He has managed to shine in a series of central roles, growing up on screen in front of his audience.

Alongside the critical acclaim, which peaked with the Oscar nomination for *What's Eating Gilbert Grape?*, Leonardo is a pin-up, the nineties symbol of everything that is 'cool'. His fans follow him from film to film, and from location to location, hoping for a glimpse of the 'real' side of their celluloid hero. It's a side of himself that Leonardo has not adequately explored yet.

Leonardo does not take all this fame and acclaim for granted, even after several years at the top of the Hollywood tree. 'No matter what position you're in with your career, the business is so shifty,' he warns. 'You're a hero one minute and then you can be out the door the next, a nobody. I've just got to maintain my passion for what I do. That's the only thing to do as an actor and as an artist in this business. If you can do what you do best and be happy, you're further along in life than most people.'

His immediate future is tied up with that of the performance – critically and commercially – of James Cameron's *Titanic*, the long overdue, wildly over-budget epic romance. Leonardo might find himself nominated for a second Oscar as he goes down with the ship. 'I think about that – I wouldn't be human if I didn't,' he said of the Oscar prospect just before the film's release. 'I don't want to expect anything at all, because then it doesn't happen. I have a funny feeling about Oscars, because I was nominated. Who knows how to deal with it? I just want to keep doing what I'm doing and hopefully people will watch my movies.'

'I just want to keep doing what I'm doing and hopefully people will watch my movies.'

In his heart, Leonardo knows his days of playing mixed-up adolescents on screen are over, and in his mid-twenties he must stop acting like one off screen. It's time to give up playing the big kid and move on to adult roles, more like those in *Titanic* than those of *The Basketball Diaries* or *Marvin's Room*. It's also time for him to discover more about himself. That process will lead him to develop the ability to deliver a range of deep, emotional performances in adult roles, making sure his career continues successfully for decades yet to come.

'The best thing about acting is that I get to lose myself in another character and actually get paid for it,' Leonardo once admitted, getting to the heart of his own mystery. 'It's a great outlet. I'm not really sure who I am; it seems I change every day.'

'With Romeo and Juliet, you're talking about two people who meet one night, and get married the same night. I believe in love at first sight – but it hasn't happened to me yet.'

Leonardo DiCaprio Filmography

Growing Pains
USA 1985–1992, 30 minute episodes
Cast: Kirk Cameron (Mike Seaver), Lisa Capps (Debbie, 1987–1988), Leonardo DiCaprio (Luke Brower, 1991-1992), Kirsten Dohring (Chrissy Seaver, 1988–1990),

Critters 3
USA 1991 89 minutes
Directed by Kristine Peterson
Screenplay by David J. Schow
Production Company: New Line Cinema
Cast: John Calvin (Clifford), Aimee Brooks (Annie), Christian Cousins (Johnny), Joseph Cousins (Johnny), William Dennis Hunt (Briggs), Nina Axelrod (Betty Briggs), Leonardo DiCaprio (Josh)

Poison Ivy
USA 1992 89 minutes
Directed by Katt Shea Ruben
Screenplay by Andy Ruben & Katt Shea Ruben
Production Company: New Line Cinema
Cast: Sara Gilbert (Sylvie Cooper), Drew Barrymore (Ivy), Tom Skerritt (Darryl Cooper), Cheryl Ladd (Georgie Cooper), Leonardo DiCaprio (1st Guy)

This Boy's Life
USA 1993 115 minutes
Directed by Michael Caton-Jones
Screenplay by Robert Getchell
Production Company: Warner Brothers
Cast: Robert De Niro (Dwight Hansen), Ellen Barkin (Caroline Wolff), Leonardo DiCaprio (Toby)

What's Eating Gilbert Grape?
USA 1993 118 minutes
Directed by Lasse Hallestrom
Screenplay by Peter Hedges, based on his novel
Production Company: Paramount
Cast: Johnny Depp (Gilbert Grape), Juliette Lewis (Becky), Mary Steenburgen (Betty Carver), Leonardo DiCaprio (Arnie Grape), Darlene Cates (Bonnie Grape), Laura Harrington (Amy Grape), Mary Kate Schellhardt (Ellen Grape)

The Foot Shooting Party
USA 1994 27 minutes
Directed by Annette Haywood-Carter
Screenplay by Kenneth F. Carter
Production Company: Touchstone
Cast: Leonardo DiCaprio

The Quick And The Dead
USA 1994 105 minutes
Directed by Sam Raimi
Screenplay by Simon Moore, John Sayles (uncredited)
Production Company: TriStar/JSB Productions
Cast: Sharon Stone (Ellen), Gene Hackman (Herod), Russell Crowe (Cort), Leonardo DiCaprio (Kid), Lance Henriksen (Ace Hanlon)

The Basketball Diaries
USA 1995 100 minutes
Directed by Scott Kalvert
Screenplay by Bryan Golubuff
Production Company: Island Pictures/New Line Cinema
Cast: Leonardo DiCaprio (Jim Carroll), Lorraine Bracco (Jim's mom), James Madio (Pedro), Patrick McGaw (Neutron), Mark Wahlberg (Mickey), Juliette Lewis (Diane Moody), Ernie Hudson (Reggie Porter)

Total Eclipse
USA 1995 110 minutes
Directed by Agnieszka Holland
Screenplay by Christopher Hampton
Production Company: Capital Films / Fine Line / Fine Line Features
Cast: Leonardo DiCaprio (Arthur Rimbaud), David Thewlis (Paul Verlaine), Romane Bohringer (Mathilde Maute), Dominique Blanc (Isabelle Rimbaud

Les Cent Et Une Nuits/One Hundred And One Nights
AKA Les Cent et une Nuits de Simon Cinema
France 1995 101 minutes
Directed by Agnes Varda
Screenplay by Agnes Varda
Production Company: Cine-Tamaris / France 3 Cinema (FR 3) / Recorded Pictures Company
Cast: Michel Piccoli (Simon Cinema), Marcello Mastroianni (The Italian Friend), Henri Garcin (Firmin, the butler) and appearances by Robert De Niro, Alain Delon, Catherine Deneuve, Gerard Depardieu, Leonardo DiCaprio, and Stephen Dorff

Marvin's Room
USA 1996 98 minutes
Directed by Jerry Zaks
Screenplay by Scott McPherson
Production Company: Tribeca Productions
Cast: Meryl Streep (Lee), Leonardo DiCaprio (Hank), Diane Keaton (Bessie), Robert De Niro (Dr. Wally), Hume Cronyn (Marvin)

William Shakespeare's Romeo & Juliet
USA 1996 120 minutes
Directed by Baz Luhrmann
Screenplay by Baz Luhrmann and Craig Pearce, based upon the play by William Shakespeare
Production Company: Bazmark / 20th Century Fox
Cast: Leonardo DiCaprio (Romeo), Claire Danes (Juliet), Zak Orth (Gregory), John Leguizamo (Tybalt), Paul Sorvino (Fulgencio Capulet), Brian Dennehy (Ted Montague), Christina Pickles (Caroline Montague), Vondie Curtis-Hall (Captain Prince), Jesse Bradford (Balthasar), M. Emmet Walsh (Apothecary), Diane Venora (Gloria Capulet), Miriam Margolyes (The Nurse), Des'ree (Diva), Pete Postlethwaite (Father Laurence)

Titanic
USA 1997 130 minutes
Directed by James Cameron
Screenplay by James Cameron
Production Companies: 20th Century Fox / Lightstorm Entertainment / Paramount Pictures
Cast: Leonardo DiCaprio (Jack Dawson), Kate Winslet (Rose Bukater), Bill Paxton (Brock Lovett), Kathy Bates (Molly Brown), Billy Zane (Cal Hockley), Jonathan Hyde (J. Bruce Ismay), Suzy Amis (Lizzy Calvert), David Warner (Spicer Lovejoy), Frances Fisher (Ruth Bukater), Bernard Hill (Capt.E.J. Smith)

The Man In The Iron Mask
USA 1998
Directed by Randall Wallace
Screenplay by Randall Wallace, based on the novel *L'homme au masque de fer* by Alexandre Dumas
Production Company: United Artists
Cast: Gabriel Byrne (D'Artagnan), Gérard Depardieu (Porthos), Leonardo DiCaprio (King Louis/Man in the Iron Mask), Jeremy Irons (Aramis), John Malkovich (Athos), Anne Parillaud (Queen Mother, Anne of d'Autriche)

WORKS IN PROGRESS

Don's Plum
USA 1998
Directed by R. D. Robb
Screenplay by R. D. Robb
Cast: Leonardo DiCaprio, Tobey Maguire, Kevin Connelly, Scott Bloom

Slay the Dreamer
USA 1998
Screenplay by Mark Lane and Donald Freed
Production Company: Hill/Fields Entertainment
Cast: Leonardo DiCaprio (Jeffrey Jenkins)